The Complete Bluegrass Banjo Player.

© 1984 Oak Publications,
A Division of Embassy Music Corporation, New York
All Rights Reserved

Order No. OK64329
US ISBN 0.8256.0245.9
UK ISBN 0.7119.0397.2

Exclusive Distributors:
Music Sales Corporation
24 East 22nd Street, New York, NY 10010 USA
Music Sales Limited
78 Newman Street, London W1P 3LA England
Music Sales Pty. Limited
27 Clarendon Street, Artarmon, Sydney NSW 2064 Australia

Printed in the United States of America by
Hamilton Printing Company
9/84

The Complete Bluegrass Banjo Player.

by D. Wayne Goforth.

Oak Publications
New York/London/Sydney

Contents

Preface

Joel Walker Sweeny is credited with the invention of the first five-string banjo in 1831. The banjo experienced great popularity throughout the 1800's. It is one (possibly the only) of the true American musical instruments. The banjo is musical, dynamic, versatile and truly American in every respect, but its playing technique up until only a few years ago was virtually uncharted and uncatalogued, making it very difficult to impossible to master. Many of the older banjo players, myself included, had to sit for hours listening to phonograph records trying to figure out the intricate fingerings and rolls necessary to play this instrument. No one it seemed had any idea how to play this musical mystery.

As a teacher of this instrument for many years, I labored monotonously to find a simple approach to communicate the various techniques which would introduce a student to this instrument. My first breakthrough came when a friend introduced me to an old music manuscript book written in 1879 by R.A. Ransom. In it, Mr. Ransom had written several songs for the banjo; alas, it was not written in traditional musical notation. I recognized right away that the form of notation used was *tablature,* which I had studied at the University of Tennessee when I studied early lute music of the 15th and 16th Centuries. The discovery of this material led me to the belief that this may be the simple approach that I had been searching for. I experimented and began to put together songs in step-by-step fashion (simple to more complex) and the result is a heirarchy of skills presented here in an easy-to-follow and easy-to-learn format with song examples to build a basic repertoire that will coax you to explore the unique beauty of the five-string banjo. Herein is the final product of years of effort by many students, teachers, photographers, artists and musicians.

Donald Wayne Goforth

Banjo Breakdown

Thoroughly learn the parts of the banjo.
This will prepare you for the instructions ahead.

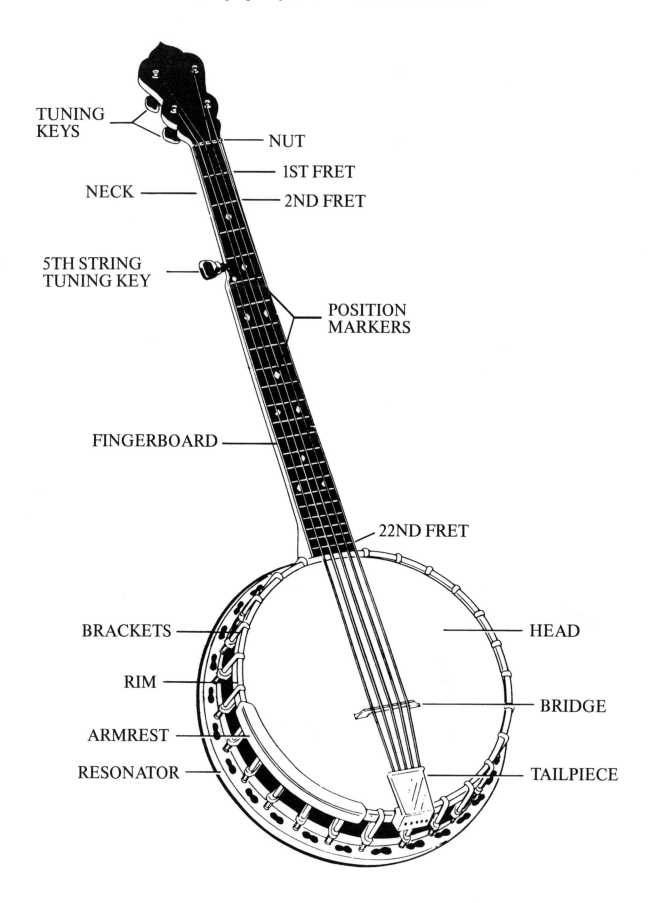

TUNING KEYS

NUT

1ST FRET

NECK

2ND FRET

5TH STRING TUNING KEY

POSITION MARKERS

FINGERBOARD

22ND FRET

BRACKETS

HEAD

RIM

ARMREST

BRIDGE

RESONATOR

TAILPIECE

Holding the Banjo

Sitting and Standing Positions

Accessories

How the Picks are placed on the right hand.

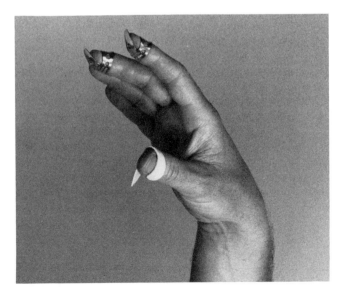 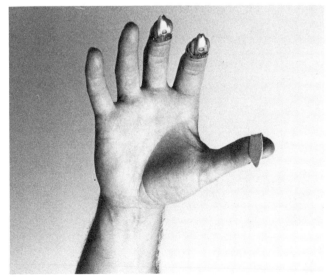

Right-Hand Placement

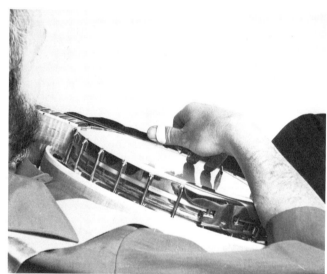

Left-Hand Placement

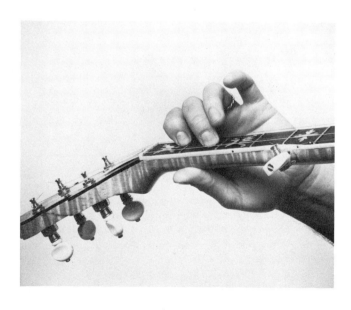
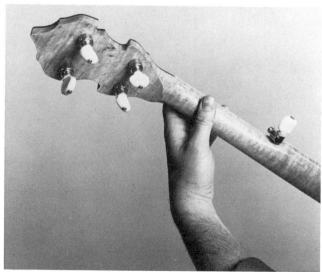

Names and Numbers of Fingers

Names of right-hand fingers.

Numbers of left-hand fingers.

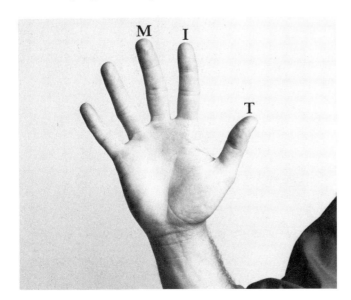

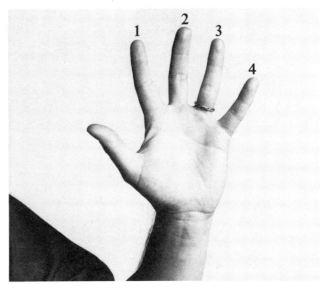

Left-hand finger chart.

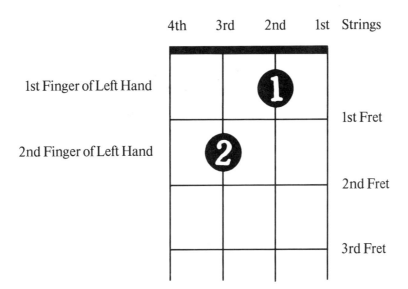

Tablature

Tablature is the key that will unlock many doors. Learn it well. For those of you who read music, you will find that tablature is not difficult to adapt to. In regards to the banjo, tablature has a distinct advantage over standard music notation in that there are some banjo techniques which are difficult to notate using the staff and note method.

Tablature, which dates back to medieval times, is a method of communicating music for fretted instruments. We have simplified and modified ancient tablature for adaptation to the five string banjo.

Tablature is the easiest and most efficient method of conveying the three-fingered technique for five string banjo because it illustrates both melody and rhythm as played by the fingers of the right and left hands.

1. The lines of the tablature staff represent the five strings of the banjo.

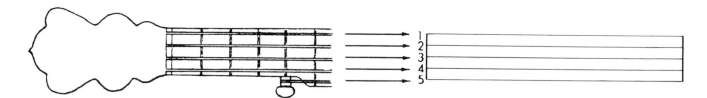

2. The letters beneath the tablature staff refer to the fingers of the right hand.

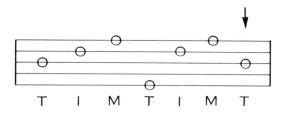

T = Thumb plays 3rd string.
I = Index finger plays 2nd string.
M = Middle finger plays 1st string.
T = Thumb plays 5th string.
An O tells you that a string is played open.

Note: There are no strings fretted with the left hand.

3. An arrow above a note indicates that the note is held twice as long as a note without an arrow.

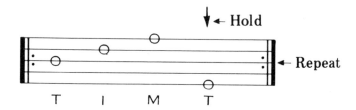

4. Numbers tell you which frets to press.

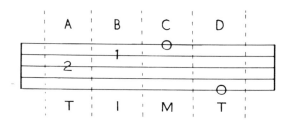

Explanation:

Left Hand.

A = Finger notes 3rd string at 2nd fret.
B = Finger notes 2nd string at 1st fret.
C = String played open.
D = String played open.

Right Hand.

T = Thumb plays 3rd string.
I = Index finger plays 2nd string.
M = Middle finger plays 1st string.
T = Thumb plays 5th string.

Note:

1. T, I, M letters *always* refer to the fingers of the right hand.

2. Numbers refer to frets (left hand).

3. Fingerings for the left hand are given in the music.

4. Learn to recognize the exercises you already know when you encounter them in a new song and you will save yourself much time and energy.

Lesson 1

The tablature in this book is written in eight notes, with the exception of the notes with black arrows ↓. One arrow indicates a quarter note (one beat). Two arrows indicate a half note (two beats). Three arrows indicate dotted half notes (three beats). Four arrows indicate whole notes (four beats), and each section between two vertical lines is called a measure.

Each lesson contains short exercises written in tablature. These are called *micro-tabs*.

G Chord: *The basic roll in tablature.*

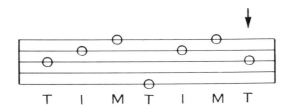

Make sure your wrist is arched and right-hand ring finger and little finger are on the head at all times. This will stabilize your hand and enable you to play rapidly.

Learn this pattern until you can do it smoothly. Smoothness is of the utmost importance. Don't worry about speed. It will come with time.

Remember how to play a G chord, always and forever.

Practice all the following micro-tabs 10 times each or until they are mastered.

Exercise 1

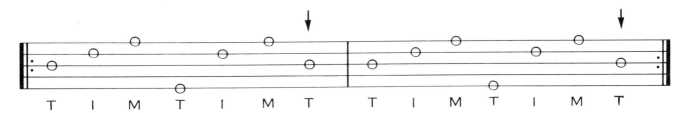

C Chord: *left hand.*

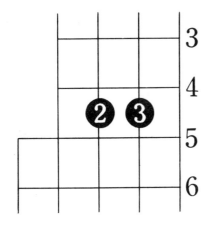

Make sure you use the left hand fingers suggested in the chord diagram. What do the 5s in the tablature represent?

Be sure your right hand is arched and fingers are placed firmly on the head.

Remember how to play a C chord, always and forever.

Exercise 2

C Chord: *in tablature.*

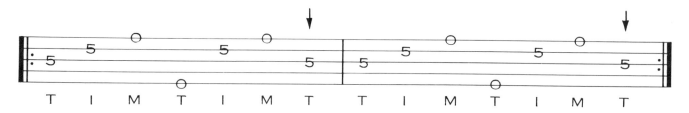

D7 Chord: *left hand.*

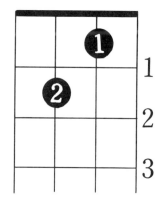

Again, the left hand fingers are very important. Remember to play the *roll* smoothly.

Remember how to play a D7 chord, always and forever.

Exercise 3

D7 Chord: *in tablature.*

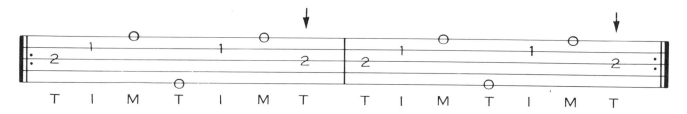

Basic Roll Breakdown

D. Wayne Goforth

Before you play the song, locate all three chords.

Play the song slowly and smoothly until you have it memorized. Notice the right-hand pattern never changes throughout the song.

Anticipate chord changes so you can make them quickly without losing time between measures.

Is your right hand arched?

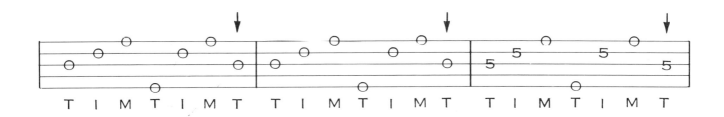

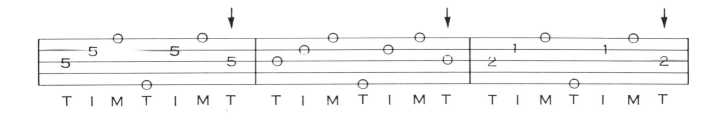

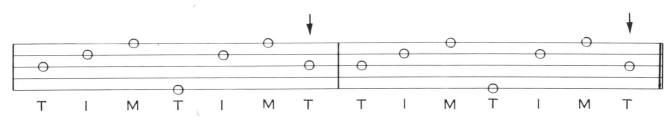

Lesson 2

Place the 2nd finger of your left hand on the 3rd string at the 2nd fret. Play the string with I finger and *immediately slide* your left-hand finger, pressure still on the string, down to the 4th fret. This will make a sliding effect between two notes.

The curved arrow between two notes will always indicate a slide.

The Slide: left hand.

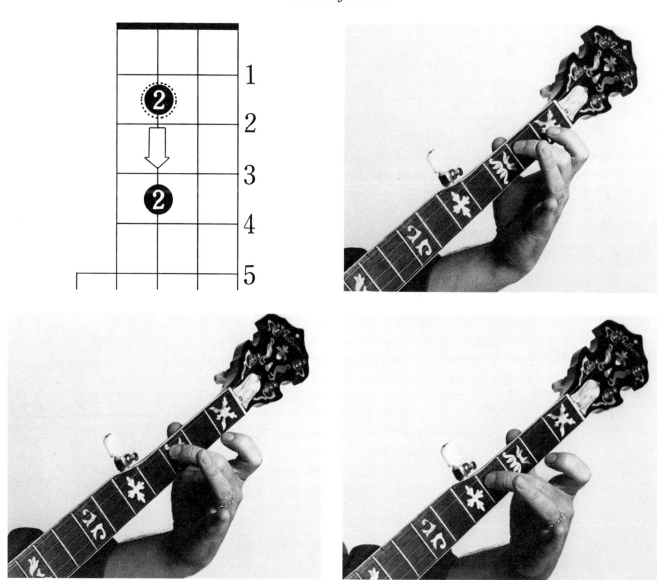

Exercise 1

The slide in tablature.

Let's take the slide we just learned and turn it into the 1st note of the *basic roll.*

Basic roll with slide.

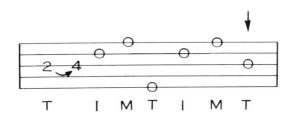

Exercise 2

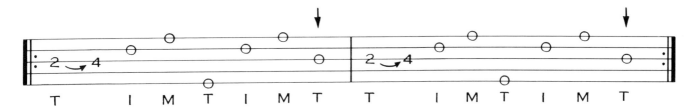

Now, start your roll with the slide as we did in the last exercise but, just as you get to the 5th string in the roll, switch your fingers up to a D7 chord.

Changing from **G Chord** *to* **D7 Chord** *in the middle of a roll.*

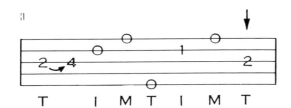

Exercise 3

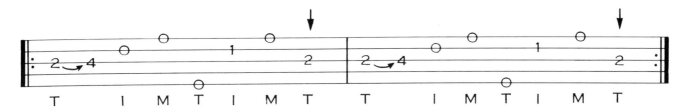

Bile That Cabbage Down

Traditional

Before playing the song, locate all the exercises we have previously done. Play slowly and smoothly until memorized. Make sure your right hand is in the proper position. Anticipate and execute chord changes without loss of time between measures

Incidentally, "bile" is an old country expression for boil.

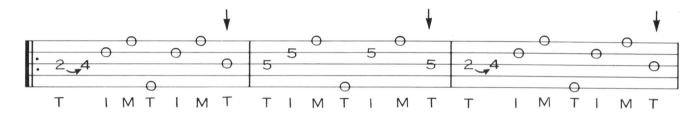

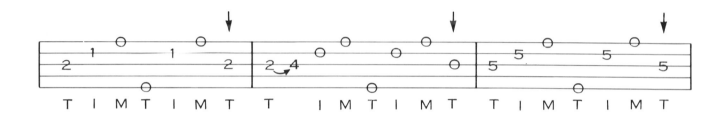

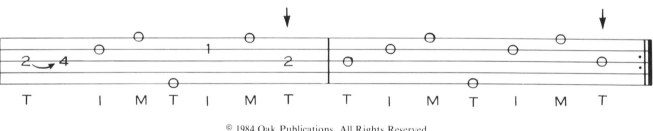

Lesson 3

Play this roll as many times as necessary until you can do it without thinking.

The double-thumb roll in tablature.

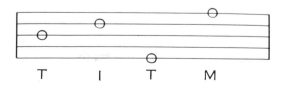

Exercise 1

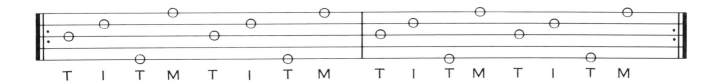

Shorten the slide that we learned in Lesson 2, and let it become the 1st string played in the *double-thumb roll.*

The double-thumb roll with slide

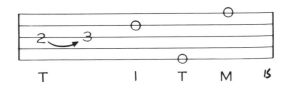

Exercise 2

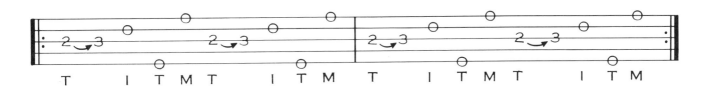

Play the 4th string open, then hammer the string hard directly behind the 2nd fret, producing two notes with only one stroke.

The term *behind the fret* means to place the finger on the side of the fret that's closest to the nut.

The hyphen between a lower and higher fret number will always indicate the hammer-on technique.

The double-thumb roll with hammer-on and pinch.

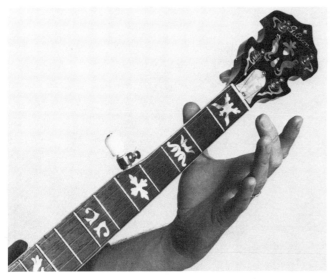

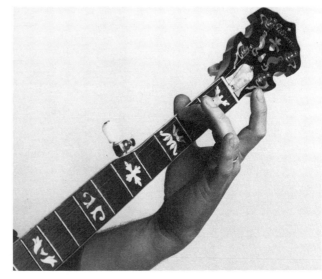

The hammer-on in tablature.

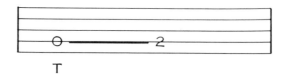

Exercise 3

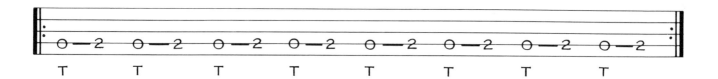

Let the hammer-on become the 1st note in the double-thumb roll.

Vary the roll by substituting the 3rd string for the 5th.

The double-thumb roll with hammer-on.

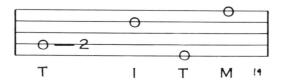

Exercise 4

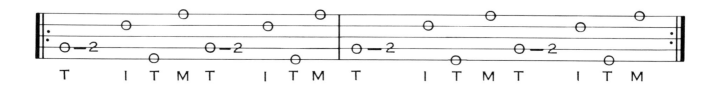

The double-thumb roll variation No. 1 with hammer-on.

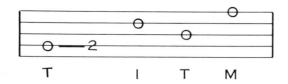

Exercise 5

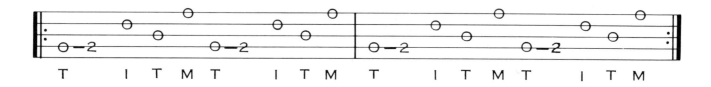

Old Dan Tucker

Traditional

Locate and identify all the exercises in the song before you try to play it. Then place your hand in the proper position and play it for smoothness – *not* for speed.

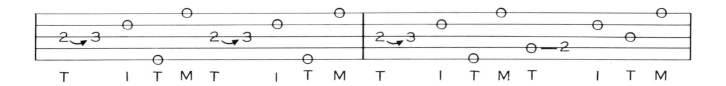

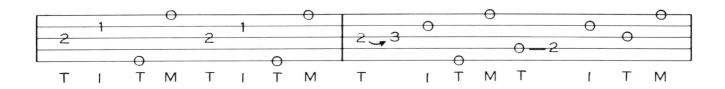

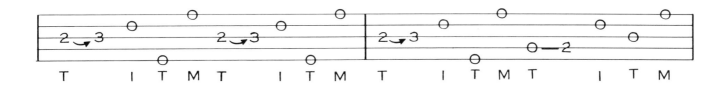

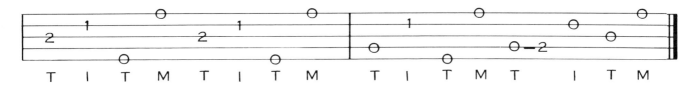

Lesson 4

The *pinch* consists of playing the 1st string and the 5th string simultaneously. Be sure to keep your right hand on the head while pinching. Do the exercise until you have mastered it.

The pinch in tablature.

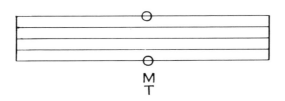

Exercise 1

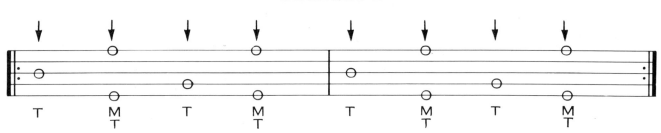

Here we combine the pinch technique with the *slide*. Start by placing your 2nd finger on the 1st string, pinch, then slide your 2nd finger to the 5th fret.

In this exercise, work the *pinch-with-slide* into the roll previously learned.

The pinch-with-slide.

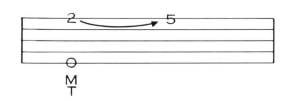

Exercise 2

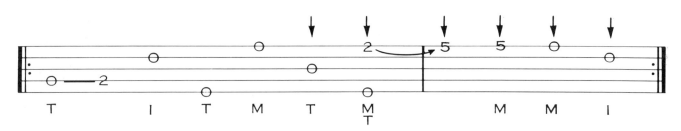

Exercise 3

Combine hammer-on, double thumb roll, and pinch.

The double-thumb roll with hammer-on and pinch

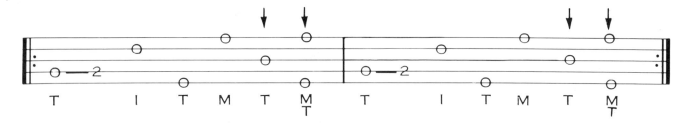

Exercise 4

Combine slide, double-thumb roll, and pinch.

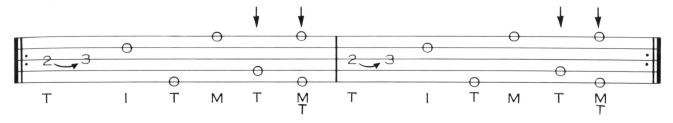

Exercise 5

Start with slide-with-double-thumb-roll, and move the 2nd finger from the 2nd fret on the 3rd string, to the 2nd fret on the 4th string.

The double-thumb roll with slide and alternating 2nd finger.

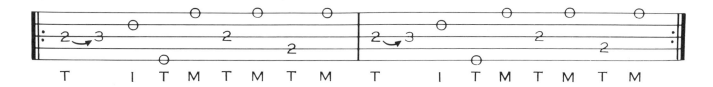

Here is a different way to play a C chord. Be sure to use correct left-hand fingers.

Play the new C chord with a partial basic roll, 1st string open – pinch.

Pay close attention to black arrows!

C Chord: *left hand.*

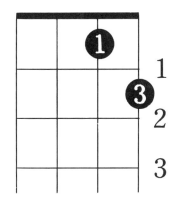

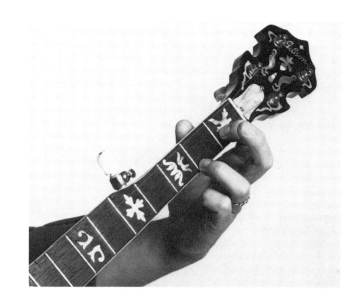

Exercise 6

C Chord: *in tablature.*

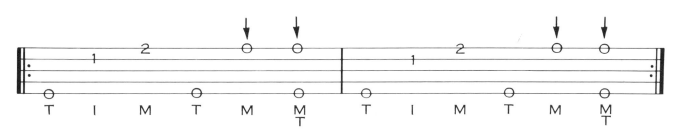

Cripple Creek

Traditional

Look over the song, locate and identify every exercise before playing.

Give careful attention to measures 8, 9, 12 and 13, where you have the pinch with slide.

Lesson 5

Combine the basic roll with the pinch. Be sure to use the *index* finger of the right hand for the 3rd string before the pinch.

Basic roll variation No. 1 in tablature.

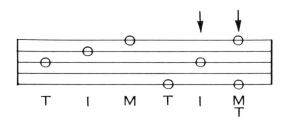

Exercise 1

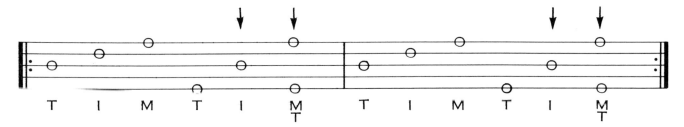

Exercise 2

Combine a hammer-on with the basic roll variation No.1. Be sure to use the *index* finger to play the 3rd string before the pinch.

Basic roll variation No. 1 with hammer-on.

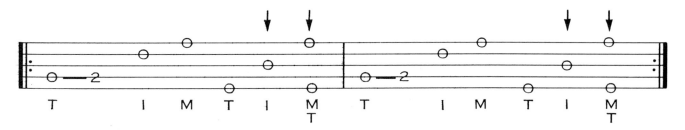

Exercise 3

Use 3rd finger on the 2nd fret 1st string.

Basic roll variation No. 1 with slide.

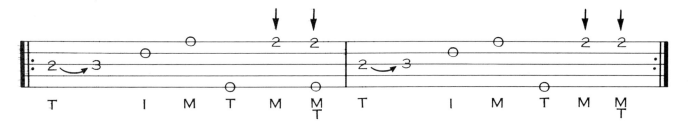

Forward reverse roll in tablature.

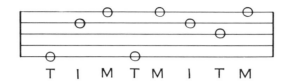

Do this roll until you can do it without thinking.

Exercise 4

Use the 3rd finger on the 2nd fret, 1st string, the
2nd finger on the 2nd fret, 3rd string.

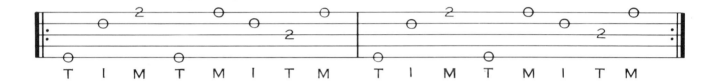

Exercise 5

Turn to page 11 and study the left-hand finger chart for this exercise - 3rd finger on the 9th fret, 1st string; 1st finger on the 8th fret, 2nd string; 2nd finger on the 9th fret, 3rd string.

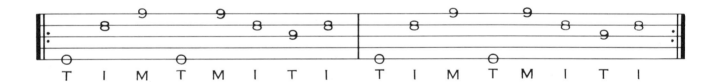

Exercise 6

Leave your 1st, 2nd and 3rd fingers on the E minor chord while you move the 4th finger from the 11th to the 10th fret on the 2nd string. This is a very important exercise designed to develop the reach of your little finger. If you experience difficulty, move your left hand slightly forward to provide more leverage.

This is a frequently used position in many banjo tunes. You'll see it again!

E Minor Chord *at the 8th fret.*

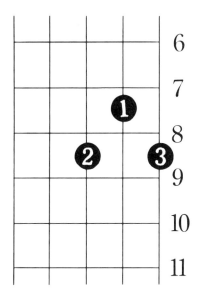

E Minor Chord *at the 8th fret with 4th finger.*

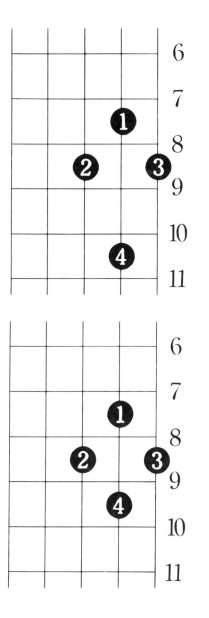

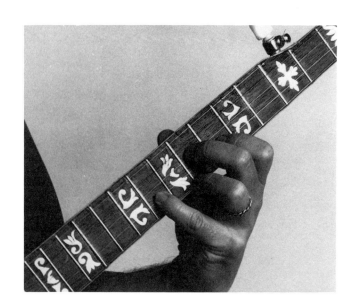

Master this exercise, paying close attention to the *IMIM* technique.

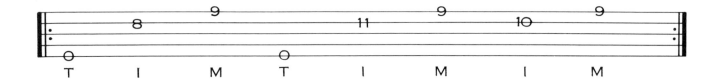

Cumberland Gap

Traditional

Locate and identify all the exercises in this song before trying to play it. Then play the song slowly for smoothness.

Remember to repeat every 4 measures.

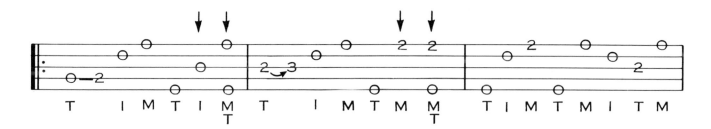

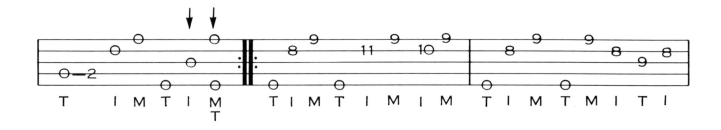

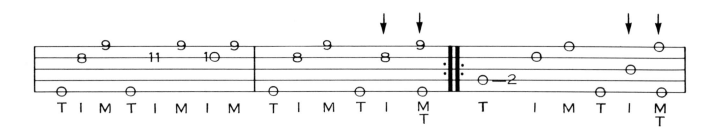

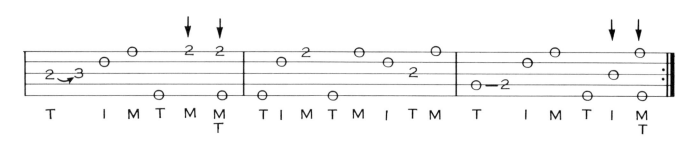

Now that you have completed the first few lessons, you are probably aware of how much time and effort it takes to become a banjo player. You have no doubt noticed how each new lesson relates to the previous lesson, building and shaping new skills and techniques as each micro tab unit is introduced.

As you know by now, regular practice every day has a definite virtue. Even if you have only a half hour per day to sit down with your banjo, be sure to take advantage of it. Most students find that setting aside a regular practice time each day provides the necessary routine that insures constant improvement. Each daily practice session should consist of tune-up, review and drill of each micro tab unit. You will build speed by playing slowly and methodically.

Continued good luck and "keep pickin'."

Lesson 6

Play the roll variation as many times as necessary until you can do it without thinking.

Basic roll variation No. 2 in tablature.

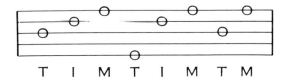

T   I   M   T   I   M   T   M

Exercise 1

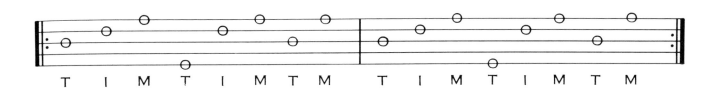

T   I   M   T   I   M   T   M   T   I   M   T   I   M   T   M

Place your 2nd finger on the 4th string, play it and immediately pull your finger off the string. The result should be two notes sounded with only one right-hand stroke – a *pull-off.*

The hyphen between a higher number and a lower number will indicate a pull-off.

Use the pull-off in the roll variation.

The pull-off in tablature.

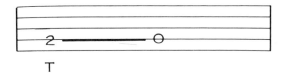

T

Exercise 2

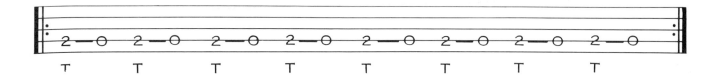

Exercise 3

Basic roll variation No. 2 with pull-off.

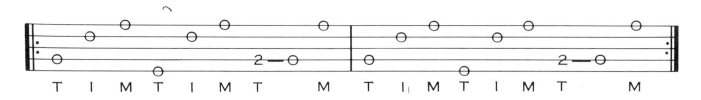

Do a forward roll, but substitute the 3rd finger on the 4th string directly behind the 3rd fret.

Forward roll variation using the third finger.

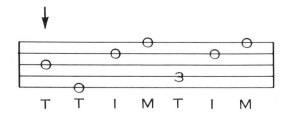

Do a hammer-on with a partial C chord (3rd finger left off 2nd fret, 1st string).

Partial C Chord with hammer-on.

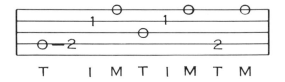

Exercise 4

Combine the above.

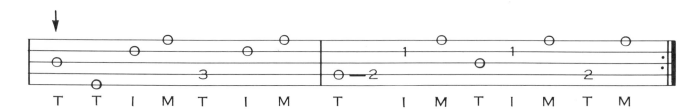

Study the forward roll as many times as necessary until you can do it without thinking.

Forward roll in tablature.

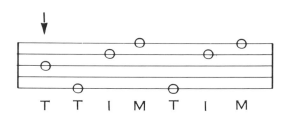

T T I M T I M

Exercise 5

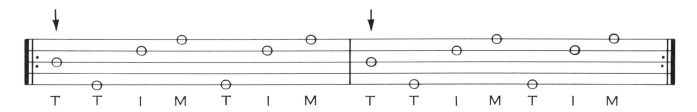

T T I M T I M T T I M T I M

Brackets (1st and 2nd endings)

Brackets indicate the order in which a song is played.

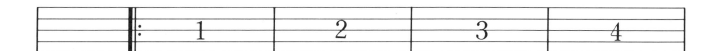

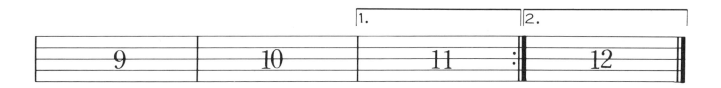

1. Start at the beginning of the song and play through measure 11 (to the repeat sign).

2. Go back to measure 1 (to the repeat sign).

3. Play through measure 10.

4. Skip measure 11.

5. End song with measure 12.

This Little Light of Mine

Traditional

Locate and identify all the exercises in this song before trying to play it. Then play the song slowly for smoothness.

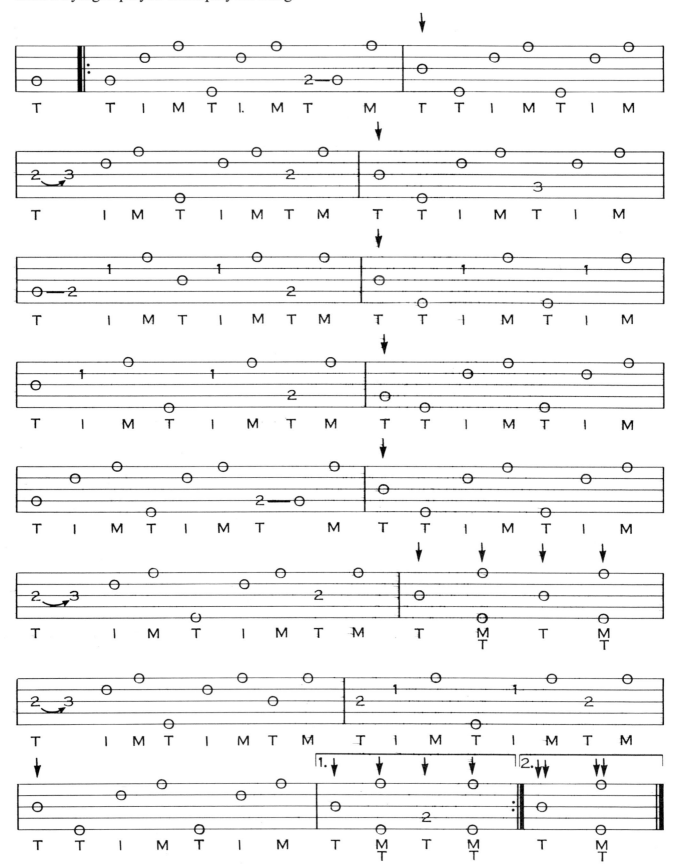

Lesson 7

Place your fingers on the C chord Lesson 4 and start the roll with a pull-off. Play it as many times as necessary until you can do it without thinking.

C Chord *with 3rd string pull-off in tablature.*

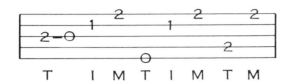

Exercise 1

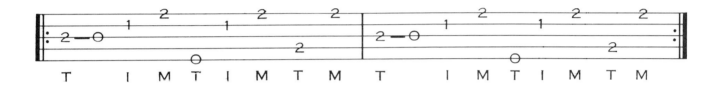

Place your *1st* finger on the *2nd* fret, 2nd string, then play the 2nd string with the I finger of the right hand. Immediately, without lifting your 1st finger, hammer your *3rd* finger down *hard* to make two sounds with one right-hand stroke. Play the open 1st string with M finger of the right hand. Play as many times as necessary until you can do it without thinking.

After the two consecutive hammer-ons, follow up with a part of the basic roll.

This is an extremely important exercise. You'll see it again.

IMTM hammer-on technique in tablature.

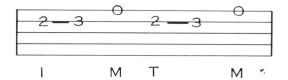

Exercise 2

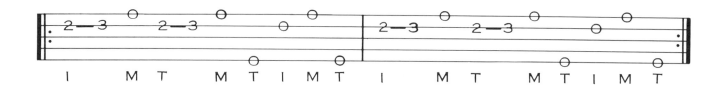

Place your 1st finger flat down on the 1st and 2nd strings of the 3rd fret. Then place your 2nd finger on the 3rd string, 4th fret. You now have a G7 chord.

G7 Chord *at the 3rd fret: left hand.*

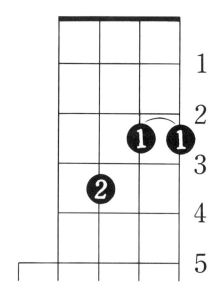

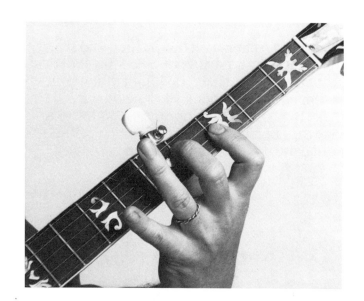

Exercise 3

This closely resembles a basic roll. Play it carefully. At the end of the exercise slide your 2nd finger back to the 2nd fret on the 3rd string.

G7 Chord *at the 3rd fret in tablature.*

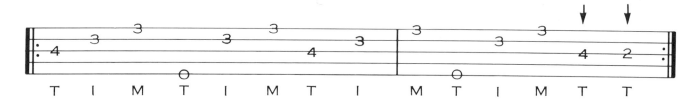

| D.S. Al Fine | Sign | Fine |

These are musical terms used in tablature to indicate the order in which a song is played.

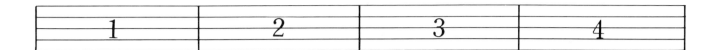

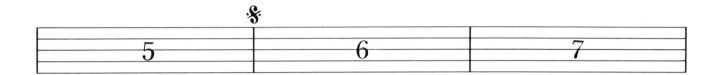

1. Begin with measure 1 and proceed to D.S. Al Fine (through measure 12).

2. Go back to the sign 𝄋 at measure 6.

3. Play to Fine (through measure 9).

Lesson 8

All of the songs up to this point have been played in the key of G. Now, let's try one in the key of C.

Exercise 1

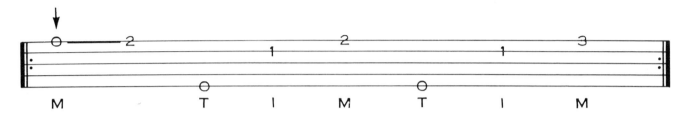

Place your 1st finger on the 2nd string directly behind the 1st fret. Leave it down. Now, place your 2nd finger on the 3rd string, directly behind the 2nd fret. Leave it down. Place the 4th finger directly behind the 3rd fret. Leave it down. You now have formed an F major chord.

Exercise 2

Begin this F major chord exercise with the 2nd finger raised slightly off the finger-board:

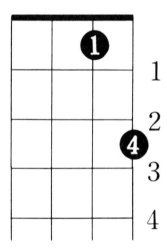

Now do the hammer-on by dropping the 2nd finger into place:

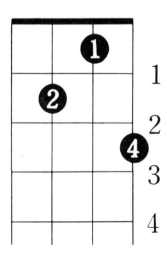

Now, the exercise. Remember to repeat until you can do it without thinking, always trying to memorize.

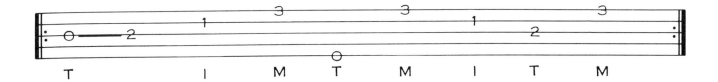

Exercise 3

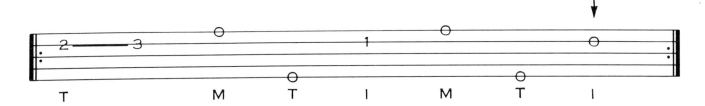

The following symbol indicates a *Brush Stroke*.

Simply brush your thumb lightly across all five strings while forming a C chord with your left hand.

Exercise 4

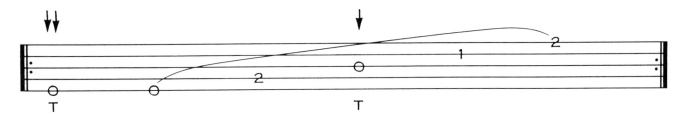

Don't Let The Smoky Mountain Smoke Get In Your Eyes

D. Wayne Goforth

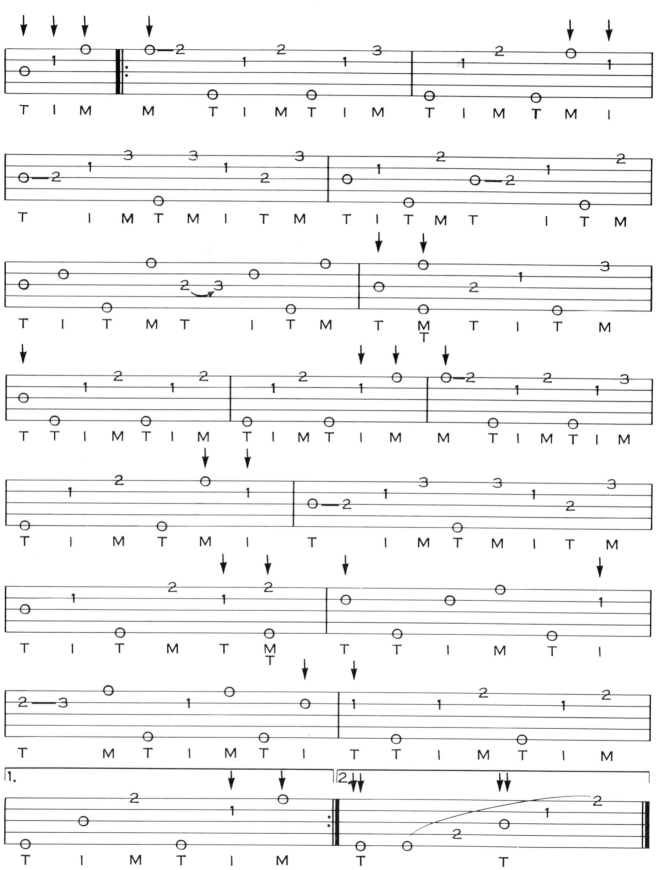

Lesson 9

Place your 2nd finger on the 3rd string directly behind the 3rd fret. Play the 3rd string with your I finger, then with the pressure still on the string, slide your left hand finger back to the 2nd fret. This is called the *reverse slide*.

Now, use the reverse slide with the *IMTM* hammer-on learned in Lesson 7.

Reverse slide in tablature.

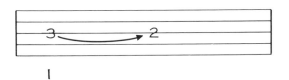

Exercise 1

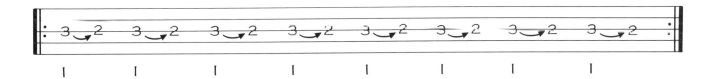

Exercise 2

IMTM hammer-on technique with reverse slide.

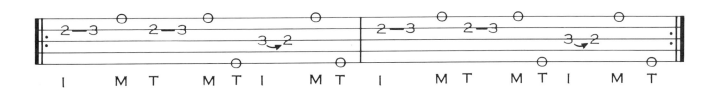

Exercise 3

Although this is not a complete D major chord, it can still be called a chord. Follow the finger suggestions and play it using a forward roll.

D Chord: *Forward roll.*

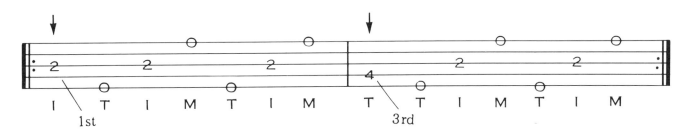

Here is a combination of forward slide and pull-off that go together to make a "fill-in lick," usually played at the end of a song. If you listen, you will hear some form of fill-in lick in nearly every advanced banjo tune. Play it until you can do it without thinking.

The fill-in lick No. 1 in tablature.

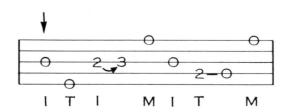

Exercise 4

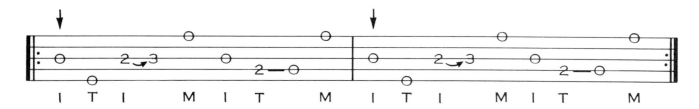

New River Train

Traditional

Locate and identify all the exercises in the following song before trying to play it.

Remember what the brackets mean?

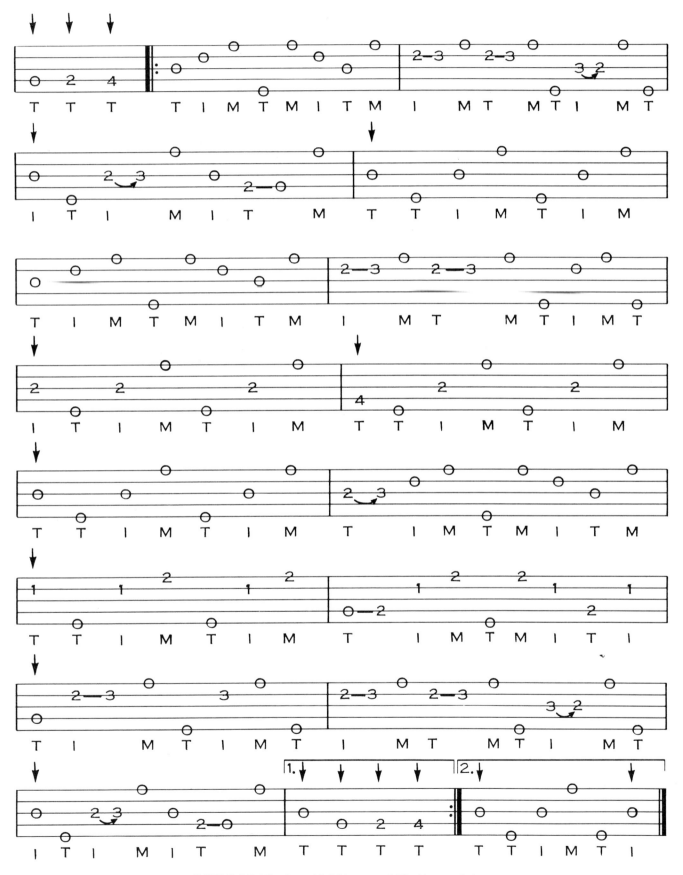

Lesson 10

With the exception of the 1st string after the first hammer-on, this is almost the same technique as learned in Lesson No. 7. Be sure to allow the appropriate length of pause after the first hammer-on. Listen carefully to the sound of the beginning of Smoky Mountain Breakdown on the record.

IT hammer-on technique in tablature.

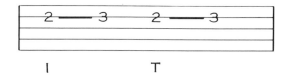

Exercise 1

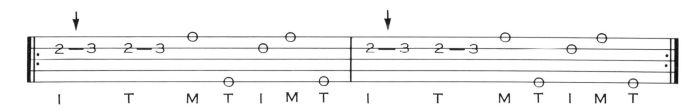

Slide with the 2nd finger of the left hand on the 4th string from the 1st fret to the 2nd. Then, immediately place the 3rd finger of the left hand directly behind the 2nd fret. Finish the measure with E minor chord.

E Minor Chord: *Forward reverse roll variation No. 1 with 4th string slide.*

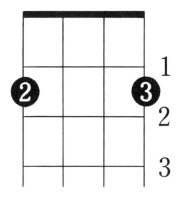

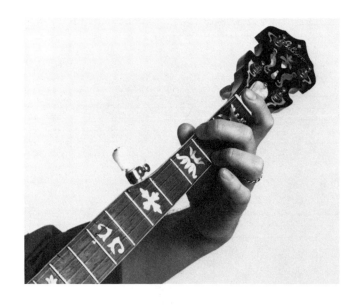

Exercise 2

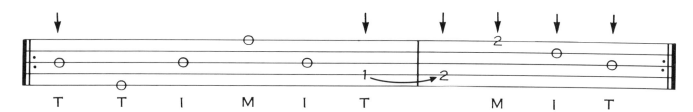

Now try a 4th string hammer-on to the 2nd fret with a forward/reverse roll with an E minor chord.

Exercise 3

Forward reverse roll with hammer-on.

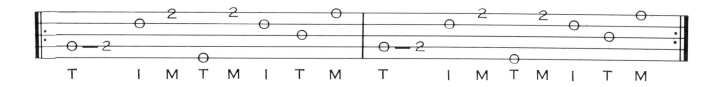

Fill-in lick no. 2 can be used not only in this song, but at the end of any phrase to keep a song moving, or in between a vocal for a backup lick.

To do fill-in lick no. 2, play the 4th string-hold, then 1st string-hold, 1st string-hold again, then 2-3 hammer-on, on the 2nd string immediately striking 1st string with M finger. Be sure to leave your 3rd finger on the 3rd string, 3rd fret and immediately place your 1st finger on the 1st string, 2nd fret and start a forward/reverse roll, but before you complete the forward/reverse roll remove fingers from both strings. Then, finish with a reverse slide on the 3rd string.

Exercise 4

The fill-in lick No. 2 in tablature.

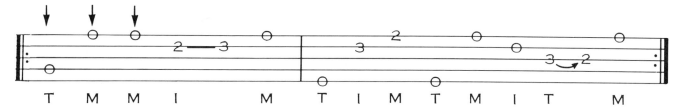

Smoky Mountain Breakdown

D. Wayne Goforth

Locate and identify all the exercises in the
following song before trying to play it.

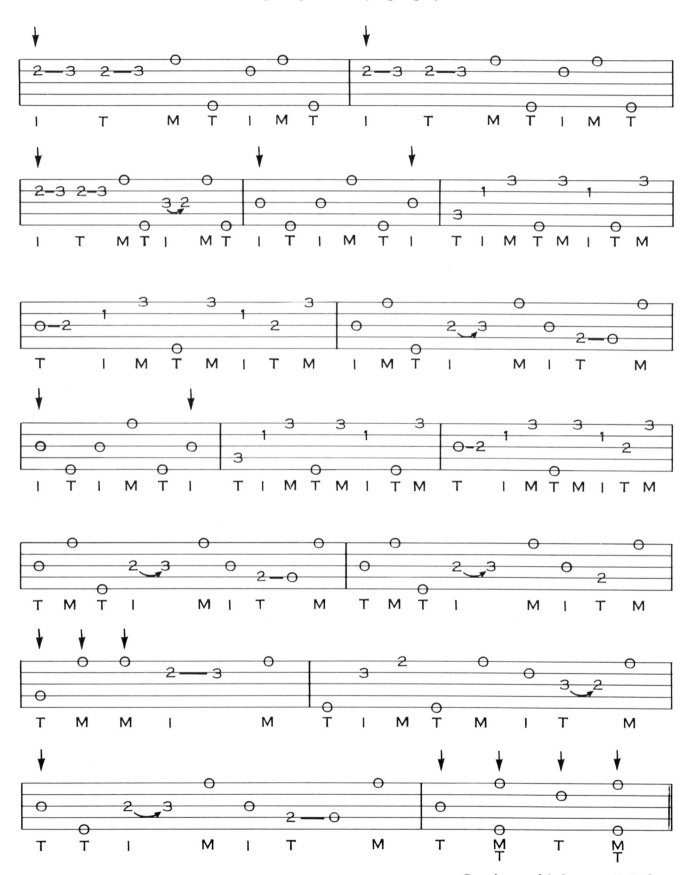

Continue with Lesson 11 before
playing the 1st part of this song.

Lesson 11

This sign (~) over a note indicates a *choke*. The choke is a technique, like the slide and hammer-on, which enables you to sound two notes while plucking the string once. This is done by bending, or "choking" a string with the first finger of the left hand.

1. First, place the 1st finger of your left hand on the 2nd string at the 10th fret, as shown in the first photo.

2. Then, just after plucking this string with the I finger, push the string across the neck toward the 3rd string as in the second photo. Be sure to keep the string firmly pressed down on the fretboard so it will continue to sound while you are bending it.

3. Then, still pressing down with your 1st finger, return the string to its original position.

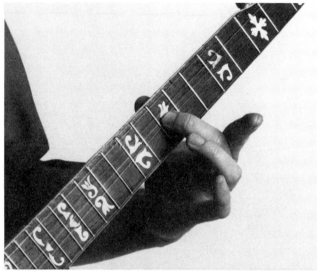

Practice these three steps until you can do them as one flowing motion, first with your I finger and then with the I and T successively.

As you can see, the choke produces an "in-between" note; not 2nd string 10th fret, and not 2nd string 11th fret either!

Exercise 1

Remember, the first note of this exercise gets twice as much time (♩) as the others.

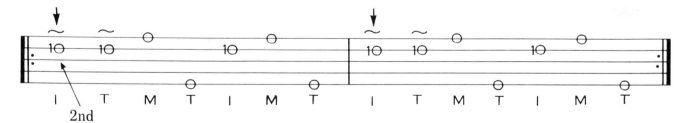

Exercise 2

Position your left hand on an E minor chord at the 8th fret, as shown at the top of page 3. Make note of its position on the neck in regard to your fret markers, so that you can find it again without your book.

E Minor Chord *at the 8th fret.*

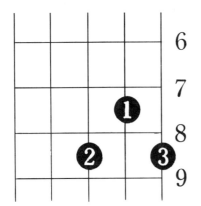

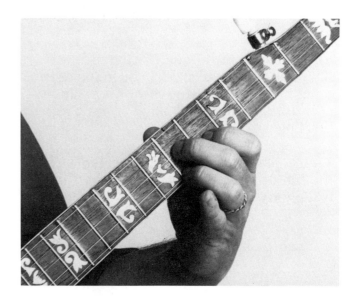

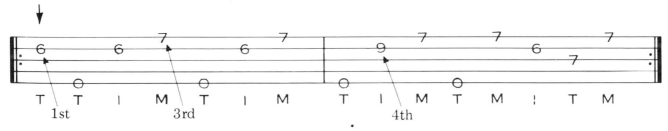

Exercise 3

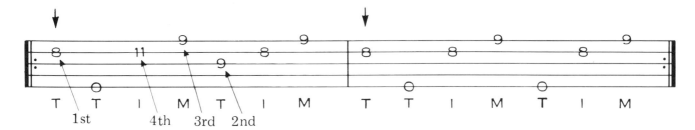

Exercise 4

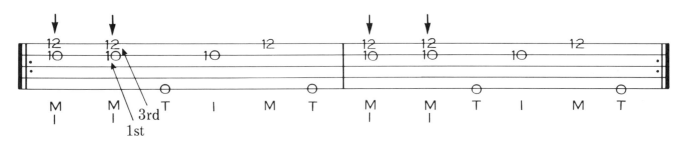

Exercise 5

The IMTM pattern for the right hand.

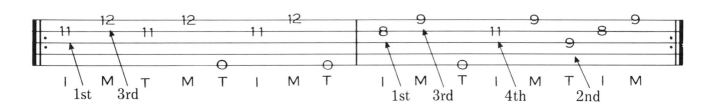

Smoky Mountain Breakdown (Part 1)

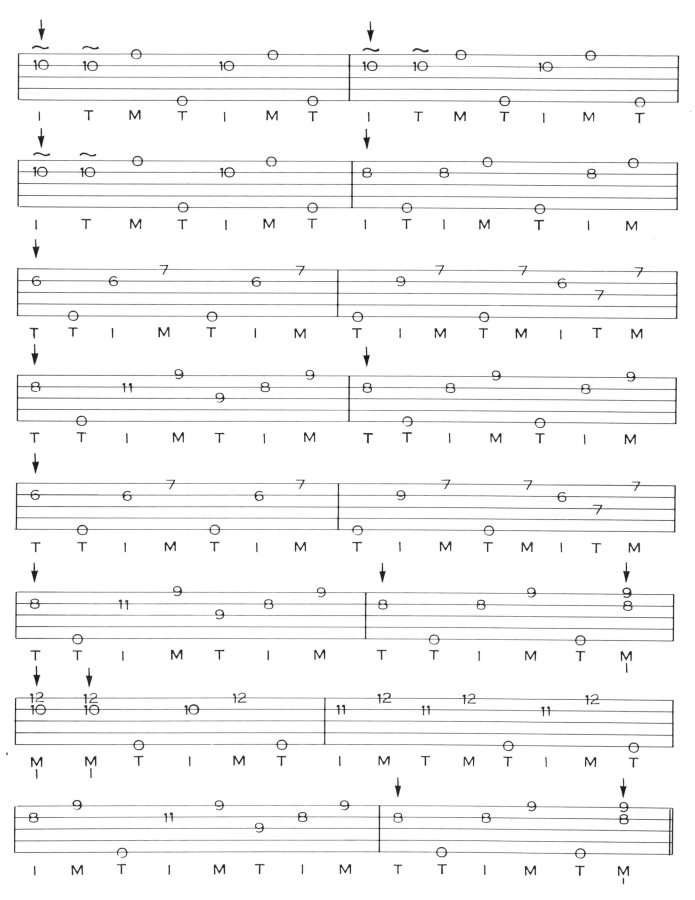

Continue with Lesson 12 before
playing the 2nd part of this song.

Lesson 12

The rhythmic patterns for "Smoky Mountain
Breakdown" (part 2)

Exercise 1

Note rhythmic similarity to Exercise 1, Lesson 1.

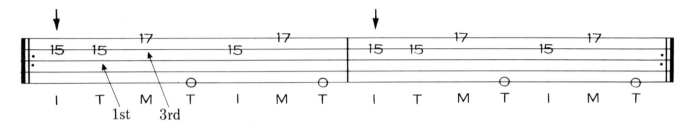

Exercise 2

Use your fret markers.

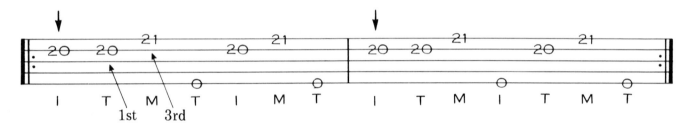

Exercise 3

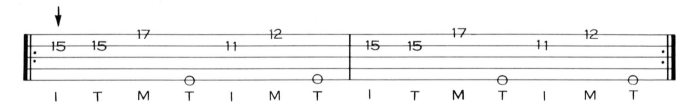

Exercise 4

Be quick with your left hand here!

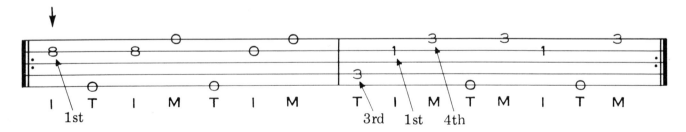

Smoky Mountain Breakdown (Part 2)

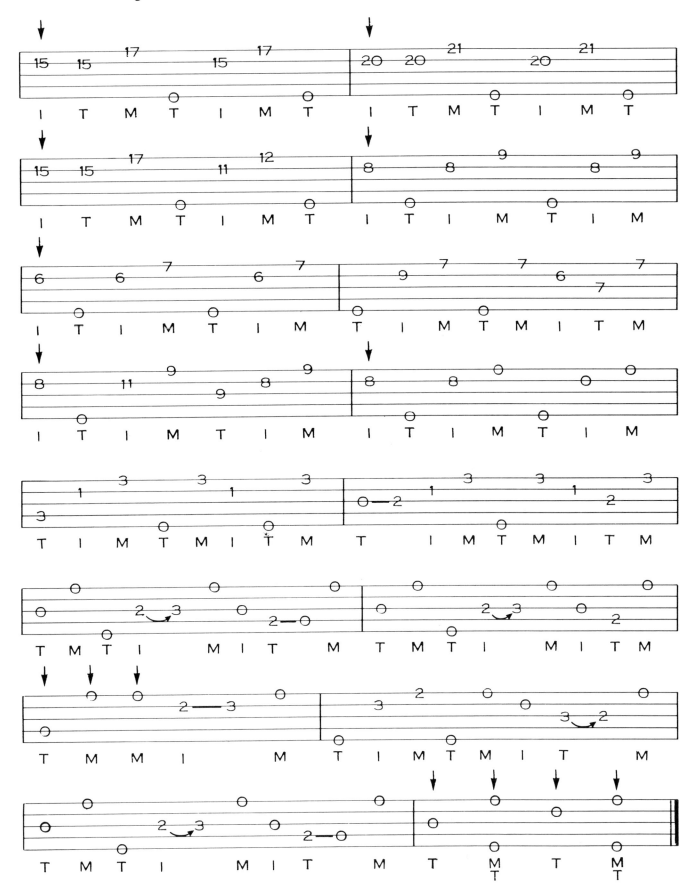

Lesson 13

Simple backup chords.

Backup chords are used when another instrument is playing the lead part. When accompanying someone on the banjo, you play the chord on the "off-beat," that is to say, the 2nd and 4th beats of each measure:

One-*two*-three-*four.*

The 1st and 3rd beats are silent . . . nothing is played. These silent beats are indicated by this sign (♪) which is called a *rest.*

Rest (♪) = a beat of *silence.*

Since the 1st and 3rd beats will be silent, we will need to keep the chords we play on the 2nd and 4th beats from ringing over into the silent beats.

This can be achieved through a technique known as *damping the strings.* To damp a chord, lift the pressure of the fingers of your left hand right after playing the chord. This will immediately stop the strings from ringing.

Exercise 1

Try this exercise first without damping the strings. Notice how it rings over? Try it again, this time damping the strings immediately

after playing the chord. Now do the same with the next exercises.

G Chord *at the 7th fret.*

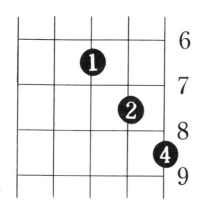

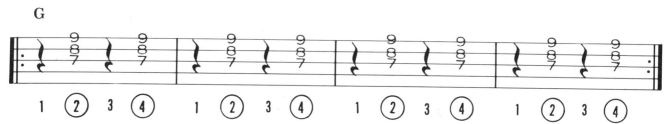

Exercise 2

C Chord *at the 8th fret.*

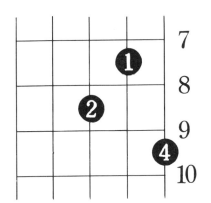

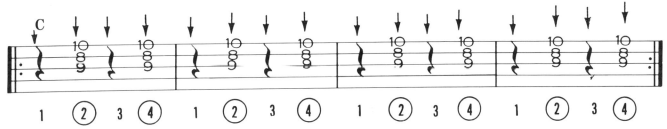

1 ② 3 ④ 1 ② 3 ④ 1 ② 3 ④ 1 ② 3 ④

Exercise 3

D Chord *at the 10th fret.*

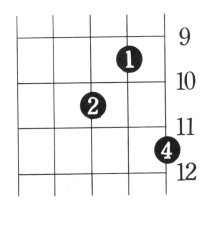

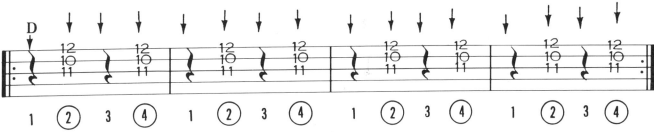

1 ② 3 ④ 1 ② 3 ④ 1 ② 3 ④ 1 ② 3 ④

Cripple Creek *backup*

The secrets to playing backup are:

1. Being able to go from one chord to another automatically.

2. Anticipating chord changes.

Spend some time going from one chord to another, without any set pattern, until it becomes second nature to you and until you become familiar with the songs in which you are playing backup.

Lesson 14

Practice the next three micro tabs, Exercises 1–3, until you can do them without thinking.

Exercise 1

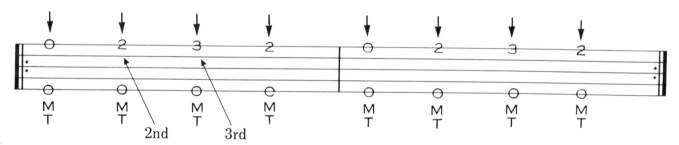

Exercise 2

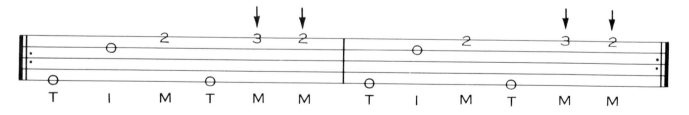

Exercise 3

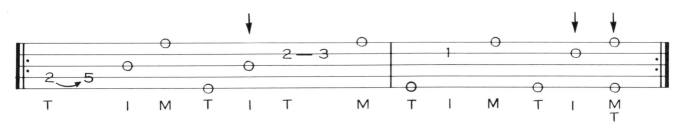

F Chord *with hammer-on.*

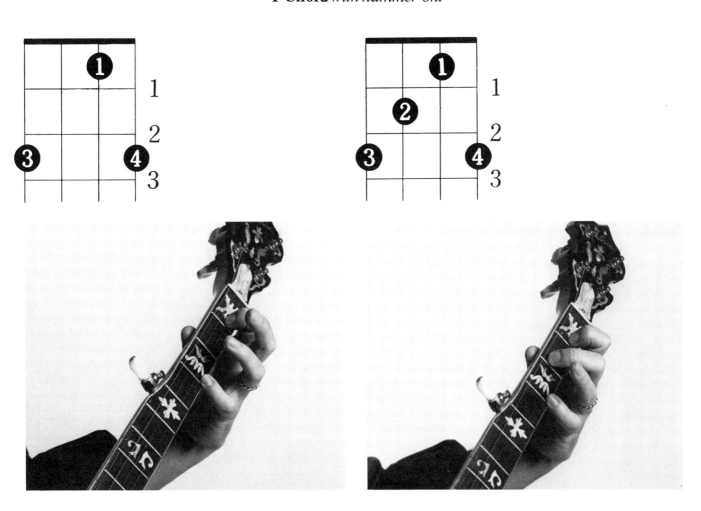

The F Chord is made by completing the
hammer-on.

Exercise 4

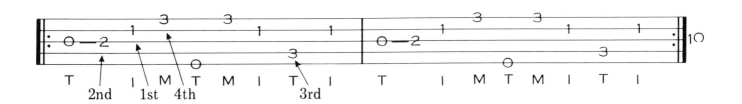

Tip: Are you memorizing the exercises as you
go along? You will learn faster if you do!

Old Joe Clark

Traditional

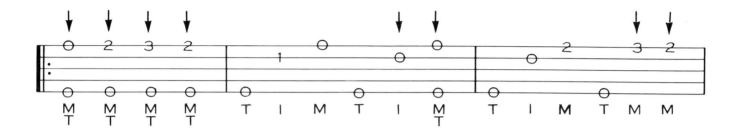

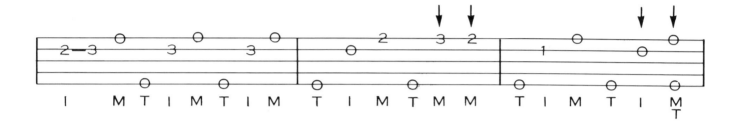

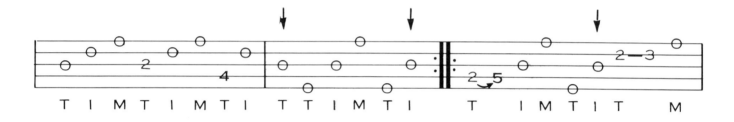

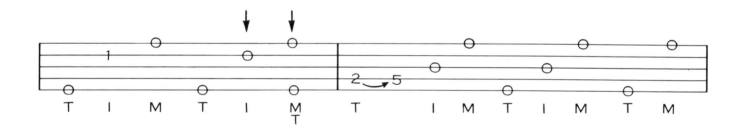

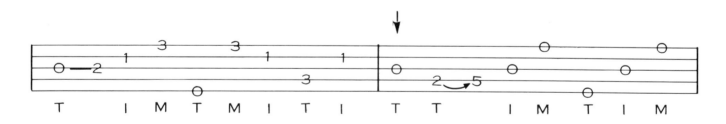

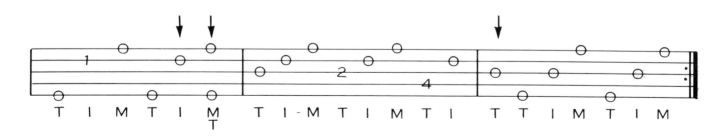

Lesson 15

Practice the following exercises until you can
do them without thinking.

Exercise 1

Introductory lick.

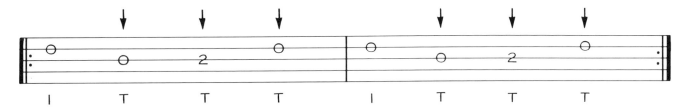

Tip: It helps sometimes, once you have mastered an exercise, to learn to do it without looking at your banjo, particularly your right hand. Hopefully, your right-hand patterns are becoming second nature to you. Remember, the more you can "free" yourself from looking at your banjo, and the music through memorization, the more time you will have to devote to your technique, smoothness, etc.

Exercise 2

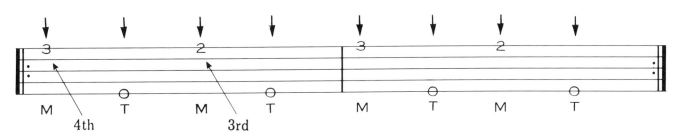

Exercise 3

4th string reverse slide.

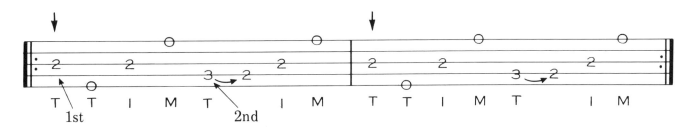

Exercise 4

3rd string IMTM hammer-on technique.

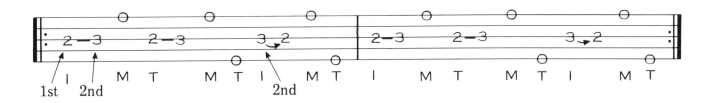

John Hardy

Traditional

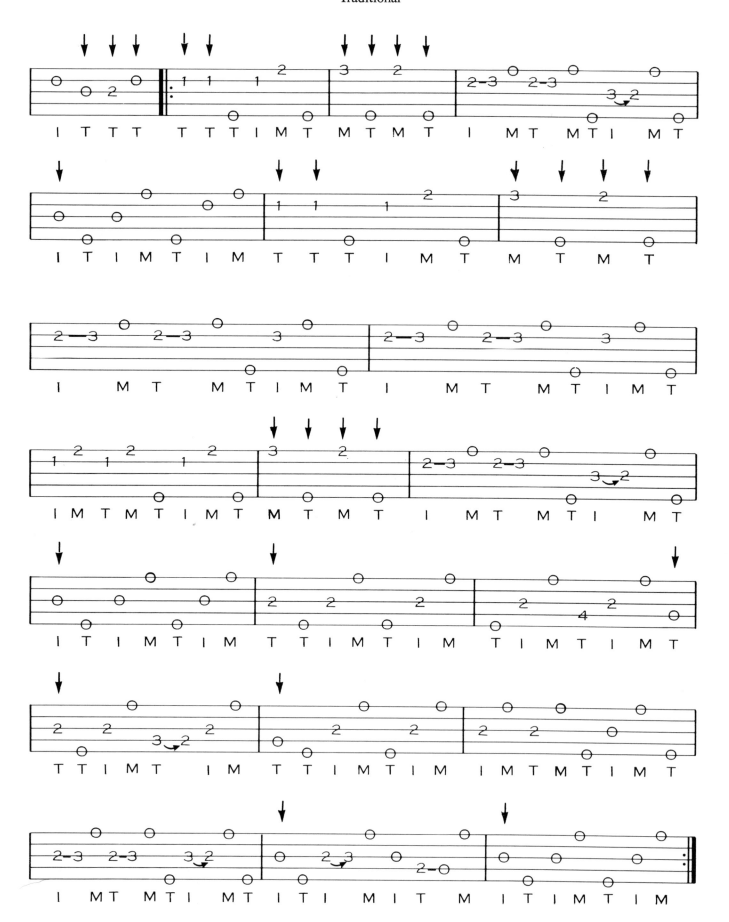

Lesson 16

Exercise 1

To position your hand on an A Chord at the 2nd fret, we will use what is called the *barre* technique. A barre is formed when two or more strings are pressed down by one finger of the left hand, usually the 1st finger. The finger forms a bar. See the photo below.

A Chord *with pull-off.*

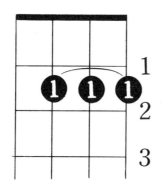
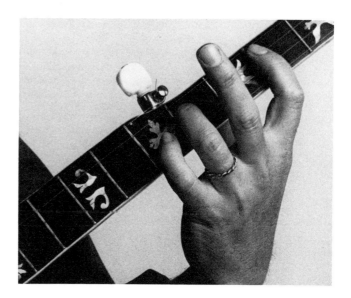

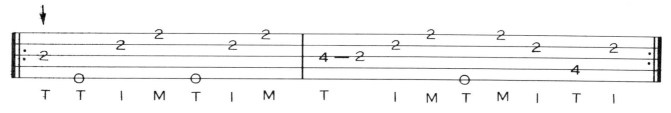

Tip: When playing a barre chord, roll your finger a little bit toward the thumb of the left hand. By using this side of your finger, you will gain strength, for your finger cannot bend sideways. Use this built-in rigidity to hold down all the strings.

Exercise 2

Here is a G Chord at the 12th fret (note fret markers).

G Chord *at the 12th fret.*

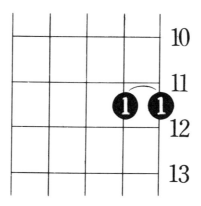

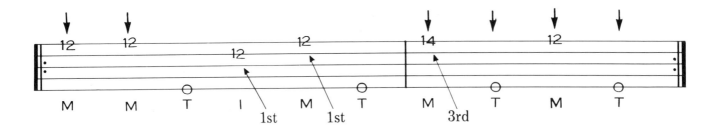

Exercise 3

Use a barre at the 14th fret.

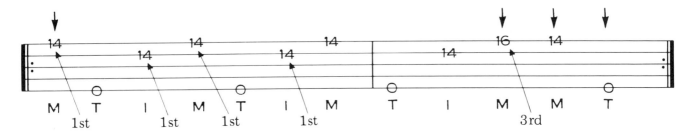

Exercise 4

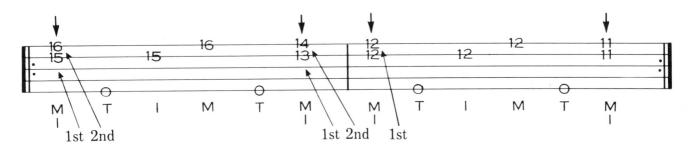

Second Time Around

D. Wayne Goforth

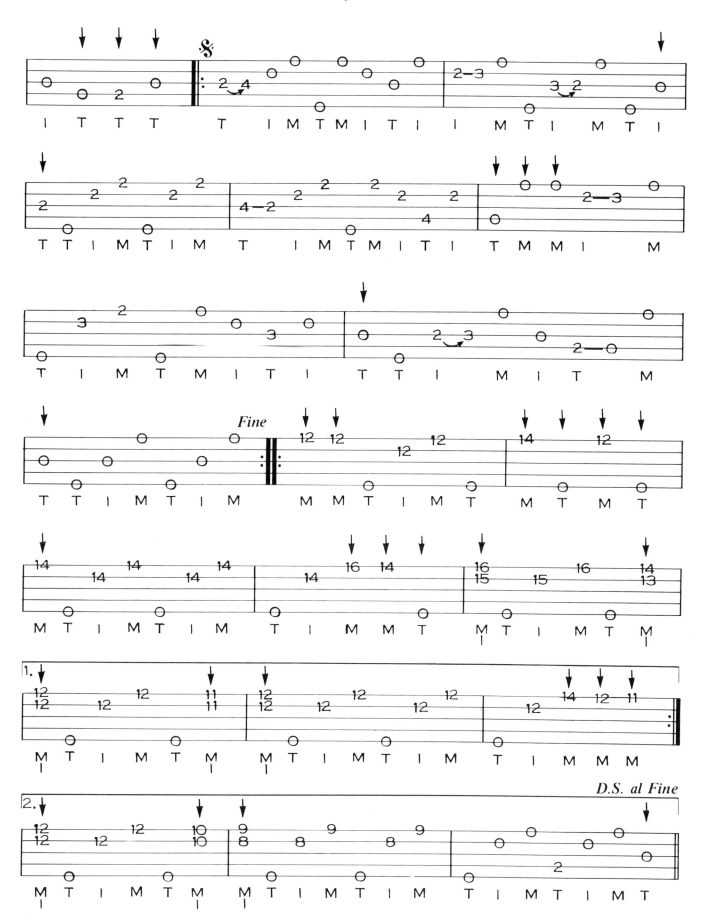

Lesson 17

Backup Chords.

Reread instructions for Lesson 3.

E Minor Chord.

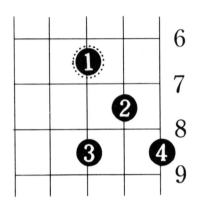

Cumberland Gap *backup*

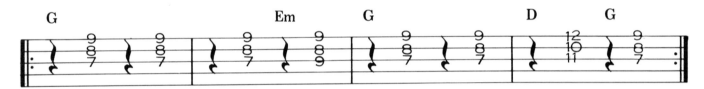

This Little Light Of Mine *backup*

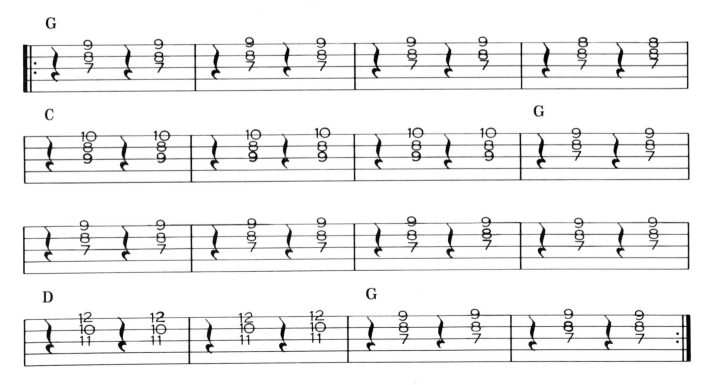

Lesson 18

Exercise 1

This is another introductory lick.

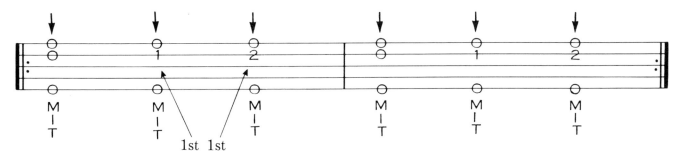

Exercise 2

What chord does this exercise start with? Learn
to recognize your chords on sight!

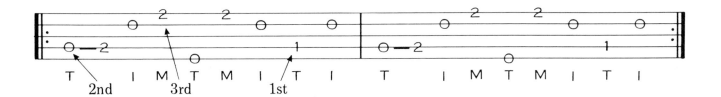

Exercise 3

Starts with an F Chord, but before you finish it,
you're playing a C Chord!

F Chord *changing to* **C Chord** *with forward roll.*

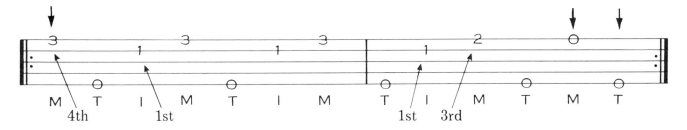

Exercise 4

F Chord *hammer-on with double thumb roll.*

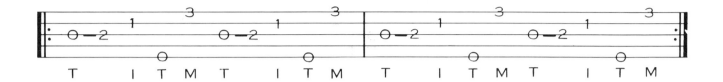

Exercise 5

The *brush stroke* is a fancy but simple ending for a banjo song. Simply brush the M finger across the strings lightly. See the photo below.

The brush-stroke.

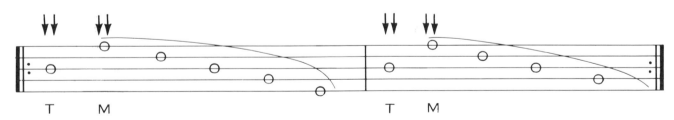

Lesson 19

Backup Chords.

Here is a G Chord at the 15th fret.

G Chord *at the 15th fret.*

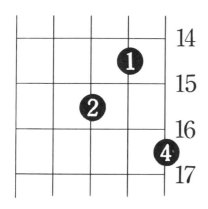

Here is an F Chord at the 5th fret. Compare this F Chord to the G Chord at the 7th fret shown in Lesson 3. Can you make an A Chord at the 9th fret this way?

F Chord *at the 5th fret.*

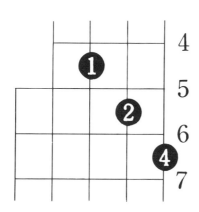

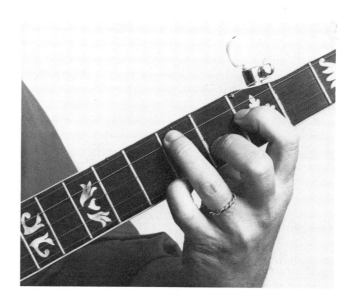

Don't Let The Smoky Mountain Smoke Get In Your Eyes *backup*

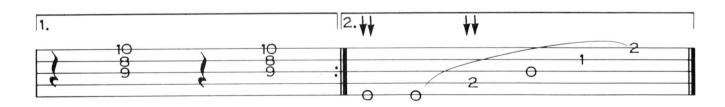

Roll In My Sweet Lover's Arms *backup*

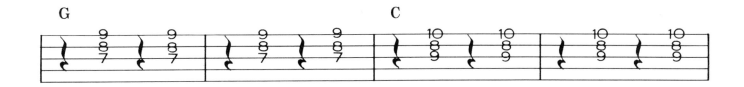

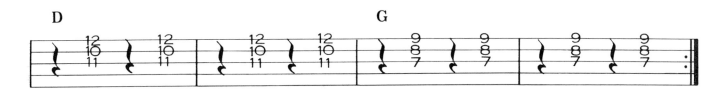

Smoky Mountain Breakdown *backup*

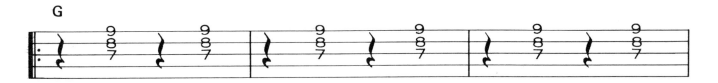

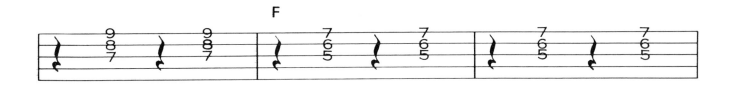

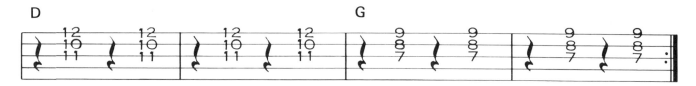

Now you know the backup chords for all the songs at the beginning level. If you feel adventurous, you might try using a double-thumb or forward-reverse roll instead of merely plucking the chord. Throw in a fill-in or two for good measure at the same place it appears in the tablature arrangement, and listen to how other banjo players play backup on their records.

Lesson 20

Exercise 1

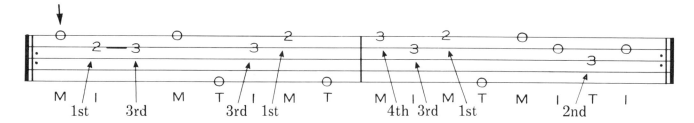

Exercise 2

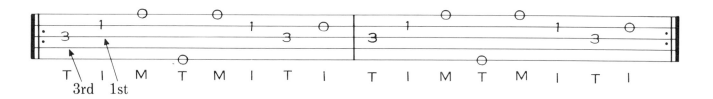

Exercise 3

There is a slightly different rhythm in this exercise. This rhythmic pattern shows up again in Lesson 11, Exercise 3, so if you learn it now and can recognize it later, you'll be that much ahead.

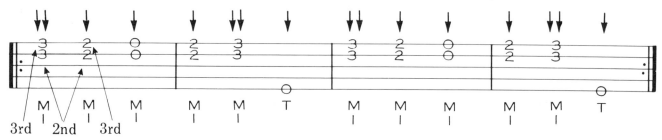

66

Lesson 21

Exercise 1

Notice that once you place your left hand in position for the beginning of this exercise, that pattern remains the same as you move your hand up the neck.

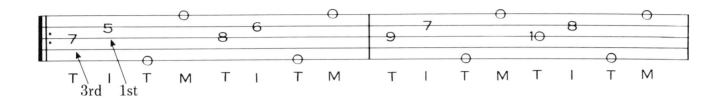

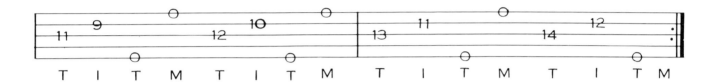

Exercise 2

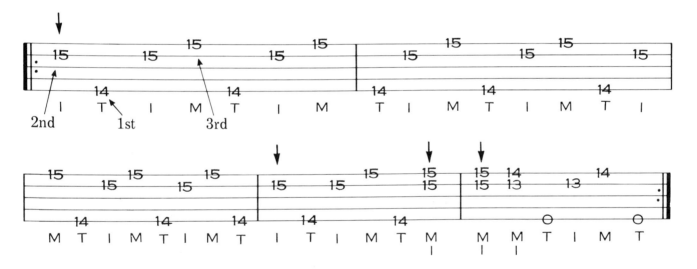

Exercise 3

Rhythm identical to Lesson 19, Exercise 3.

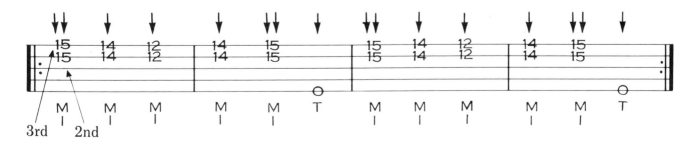

Lesson 22

Review Exercises on Backup Techniques and Chords.

Exercise 1

The fill-in lick No. 1.

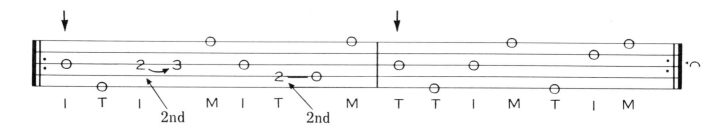

Exercise 2

E Chord *at the 4th fret.*

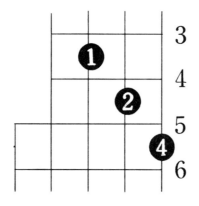

Exercise 3

Here is an illustration of an A Chord at the 9th fret. Notice how these last two chords relate to the G Chord at the 7th fret found in Lesson 3.

A Chord *at the 9th fret.*

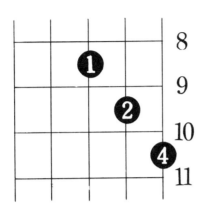

Remember: Become familiar with the chords and changing from one to the other. Anticipate the changes.

Old Joe Clark *backup*

Notice on the next two songs that a fill-in lick is used on the "turnaround;" this is where the song *turns around* to start over. It is pretty much standard procedure on all backup playing. Practice with a guitar-playing friend and take turns playing the lead.

John Hardy *backup*

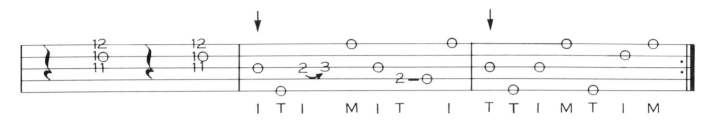

Second Time Around *backup*

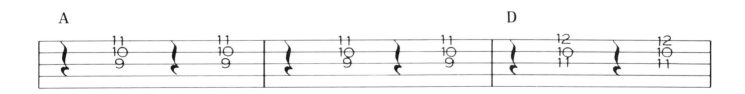

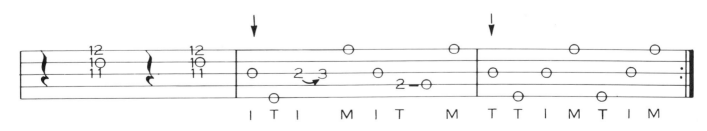

From time to time you will be required to play a song in a key such as A, B, E, etc. in order to accommodate the voices or playing styles of the people you pick with. This is no great problem if you use a capo. You can "capo up" to a higher key and still maintain your standard G, C, or D tuning, playing the song just the way you learned it.

By now, you should be ready to have a 5th string capo installed in your local music studio.

As a rule, for every fret you move your regular capo up the neck, you slide your 5th string capo up the same number.

Capo placement for key of B.

Fifth String Capo   *Capo*

Therefore, if your regular capo is placed on the 4th fret, your 5th string capo would also be moved up 4 frets to the 9th fret (see photo above).

Here is a chart of the capo placements for the standard G, C, and D tunings for the first 5 frets.

Open	G	C	D
1st fret	G# (A♭)	C# (D♭)	D# (E♭)
2nd fret	A	D	E
3rd fret	B♭ (A#)	D# (E♭)	F
4th fret	B	E	F# (E♭)
5th fret	C	F	G

Place your capos directly behind the fret, as you would your finger. Make sure they fit snugly.

Lesson 23

In this lesson you may notice some of the licks you've learned being used in new combinations.

Exercise 1

Watch your ↓'s.

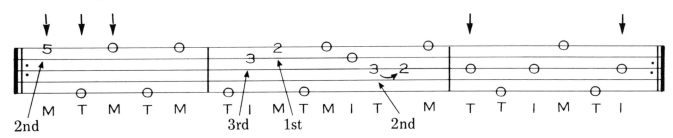

Exercise 2

Slowly, at first, then build up speed.

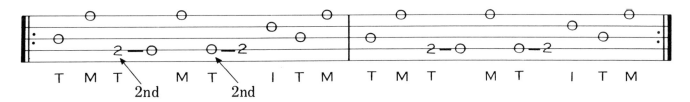

Exercise 3

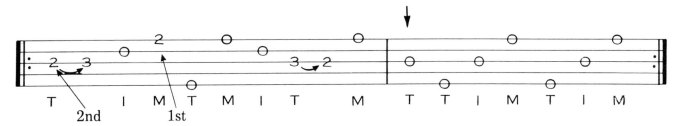

Tip: When playing a slide, either forward or reverse, try to move *just the 1st finger* of your left hand. Keep the rest of your hand relatively still.

Don't waste any more movement than is necessary.

Exercise 4

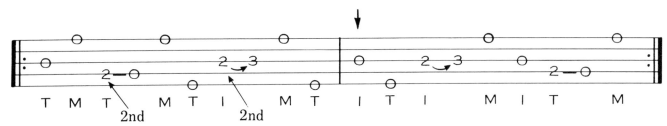

If on John Henry, or any other song, you run into a particular passage that is giving you trouble:

1. Try playing the song "in your own head."

2. Practice the problem passage by itself slowly, then with the measures which occur before and after it in the song.

3. *Gradually* increase speed.

John Henry

Traditional

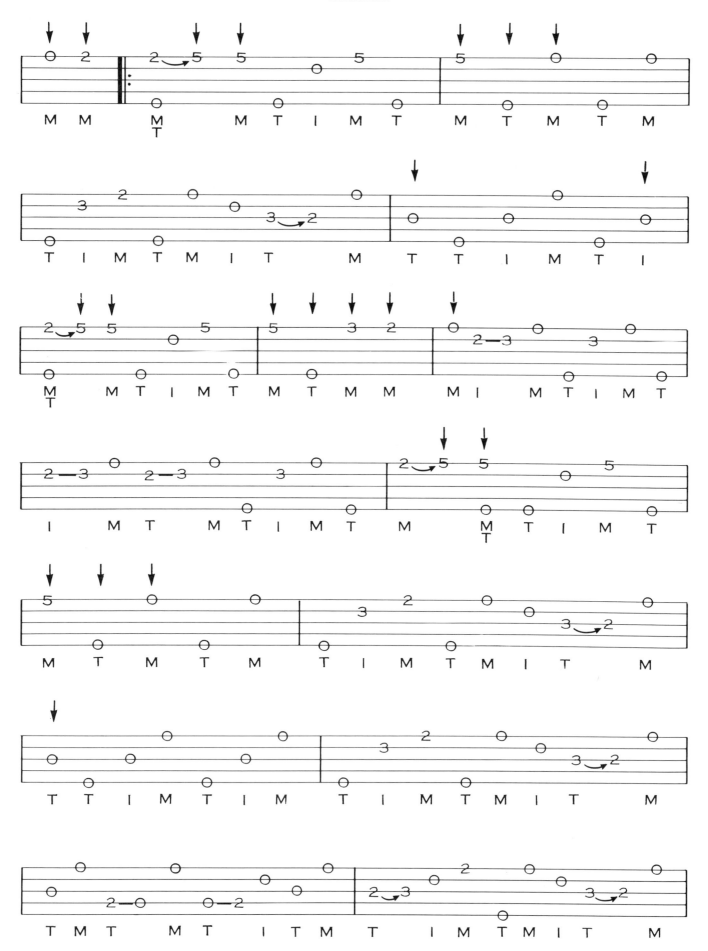

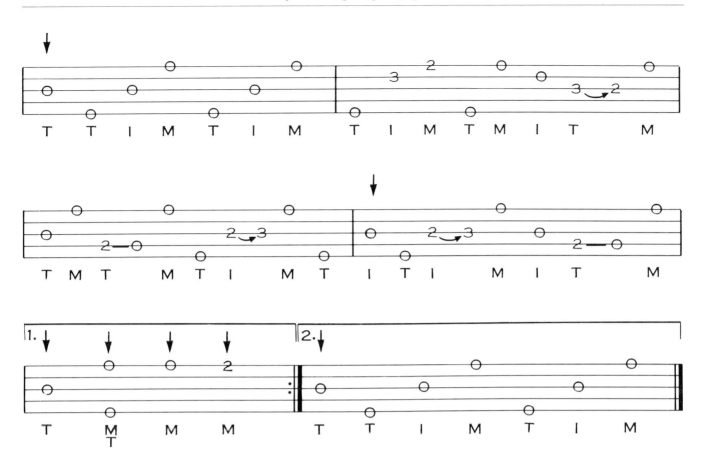

Lesson 24

The key to "Banjo Sentinel" is the left-hand positioning and fingering. Master this and the rest is easy.

Exercise 1

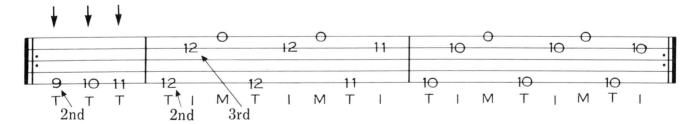

Exercise 2

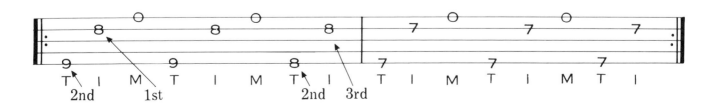

Banjo Sentinel

D. Wayne Goforth

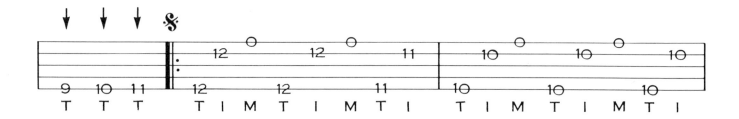

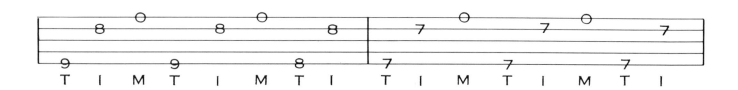

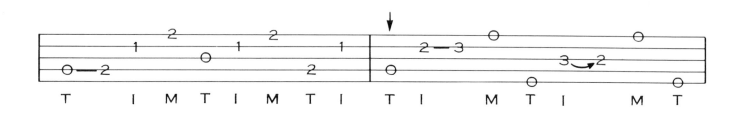

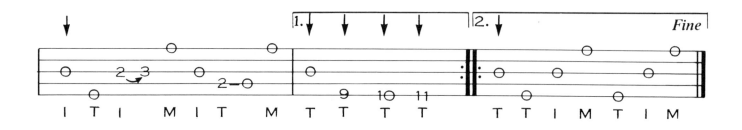

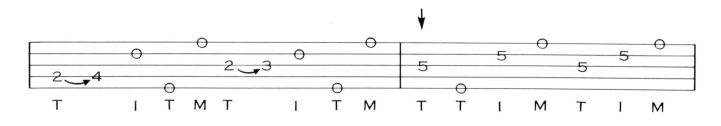

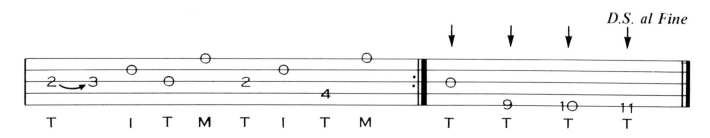

Lesson 25

Exercise 1

Listen to what you're doing.

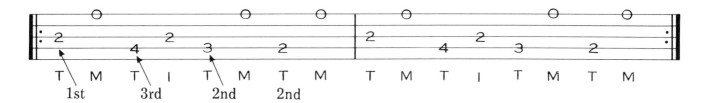

Exercise 2

The hammer-on pull-off technique.

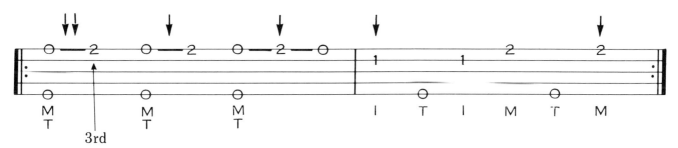

Exercise 3

Notice the IMTM pattern.

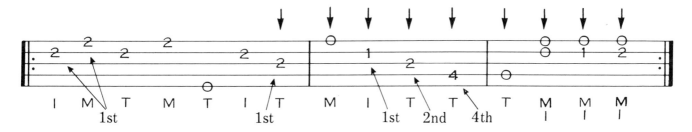

Exercise 4

The fill-in lick No. 2

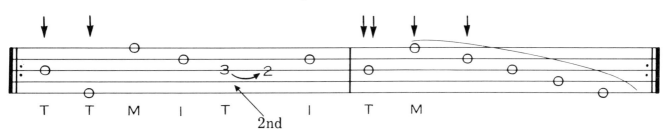

Did you know that many of the fill-in licks are interchangeable? It's all a matter of what sounds best to you.

When You And I Were Young, Maggie

George W. Johnson & J. A. Butterfield

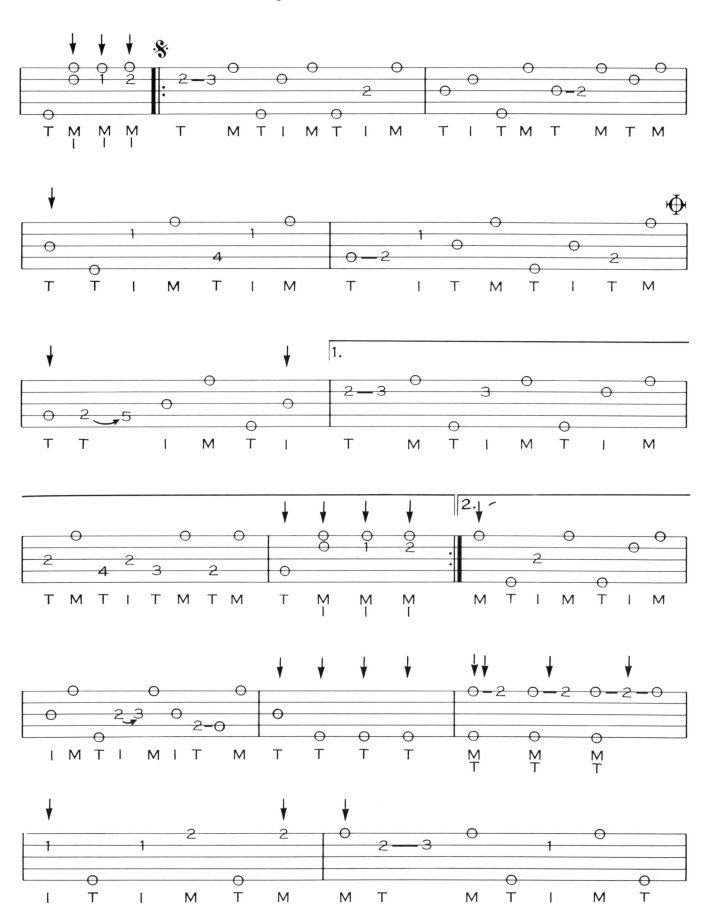

D.S. al Coda

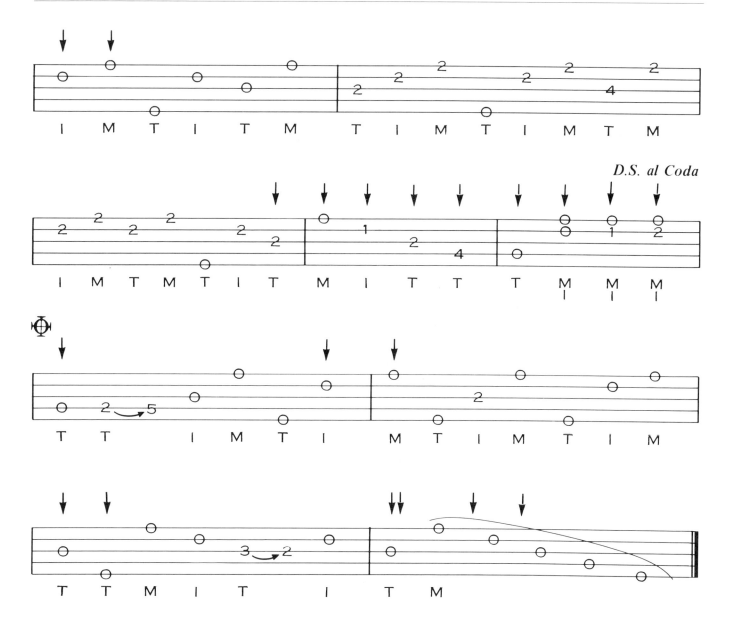

Lesson 26

"Devil's Dream" is your first introduction to the chromatic style of playing, a melodic style in which the notes fall into a chromatic scale.

The main difficulty students have with this style is that quite often the lower sounding strings are fretted in such a way as to make them play higher notes than, say, the first or second string. It takes a while to get used to this.

When learning chromatics, be sure and pay very close attention to the left-hand fingering,

as it is of critical importance. It may seem a little strange at first, but after you get used to it, and begin to recognize various chromatic patterns as they appear, it can provide a welcome change from the way you've learned to play so far.

Be sure and use your ears while you perfect these exercises. It's important to learn how a chromatic scale sounds.

Exercise 1

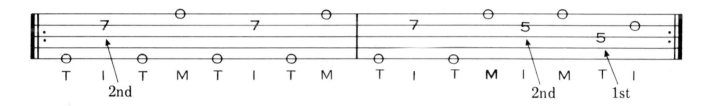

Exercise 2

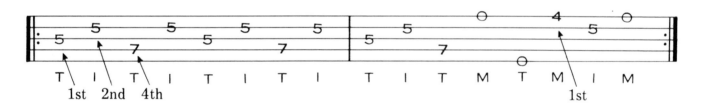

Exercise 3

Inside roll.

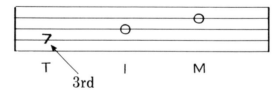

This is called an *inside roll* as it is done on the inside strings.

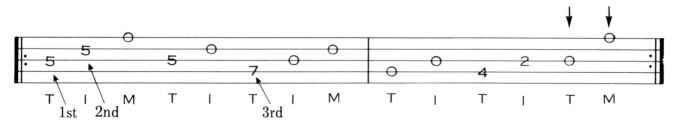

Exercise 4

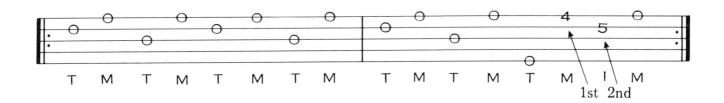

Devil's Dream

Traditional

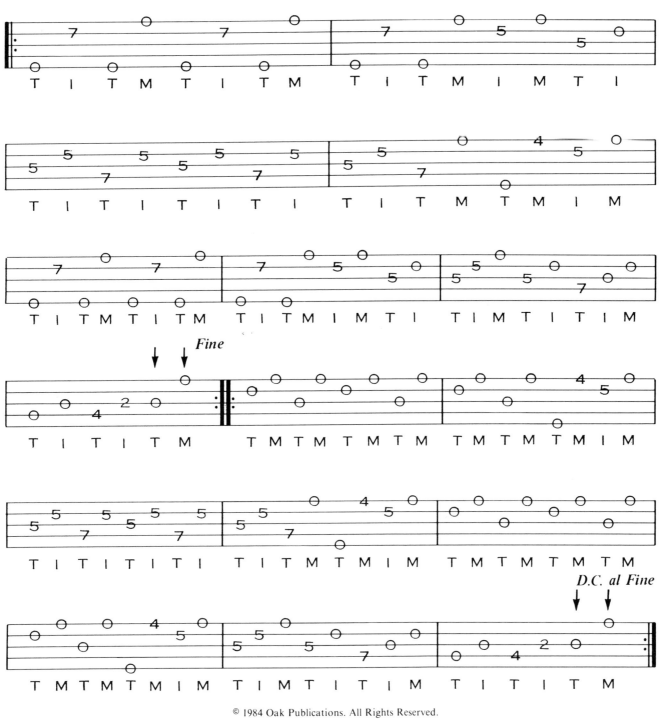

Lesson 27

If this song sounds slightly different to you, it's because it is in 3/4 or waltz time. It has only 3 beats per measure instead of the 4 you are accustomed to. Each measure is counted out like this:

One, two, three/*one,* two, three; the accent being on the first beat of each measure.

Place your banjo in C tuning by lowering the 4th string to where, at the 7th fret, it sounds identical to the open 3rd string.

Exercise 1

Try and feel the 3/4 time.

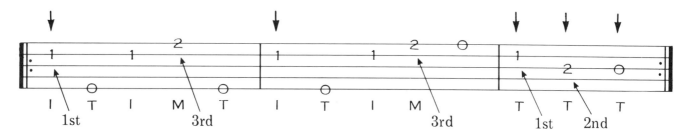

Exercise 2

A Minor Chord *with hammer-on.*

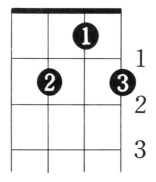

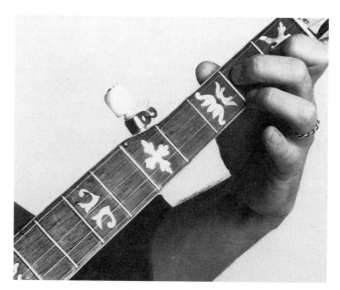

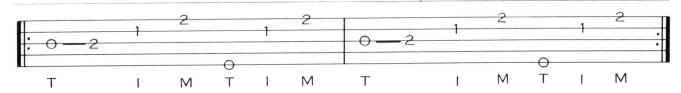

The hammer-on completes the A minor Chord.

Exercise 3

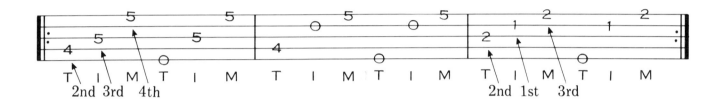

Exercise 4

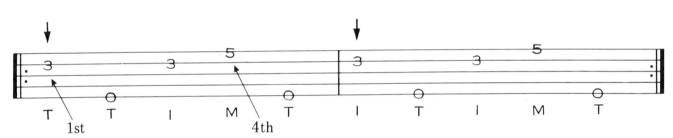

Lesson 28

To put your banjo in D tuning, follow these instructions:

A. Press 4th string at 4th fret.
B. Play 3rd string open.
C. Lower 3rd string until it sounds like 4th string, 4th fret.
D. Press 3rd string at 3rd fret.
E. Play second string open.

F. Lower 2nd string until it sounds like 3rd string, 3rd fret.
G. Press 1st string at 4th fret.
H. Play 5th string open.
I. Lower 5th string until it sounds like 1st string, 4th fret.

The notes within the measures should sound the same.

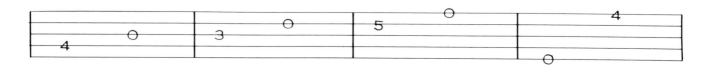

Exercise 1

Closed position pull-off.

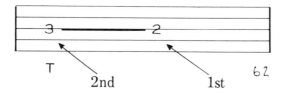

This is a closed position pull-off as it is not to an open string.

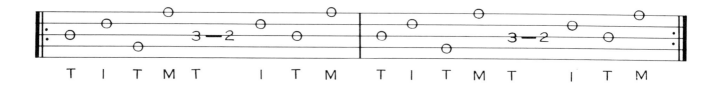

Exercise 2

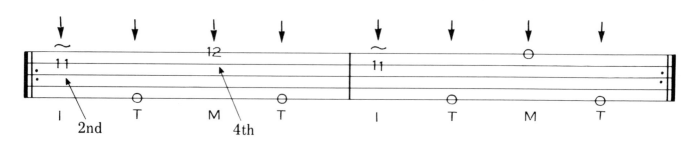

Exercise 3

Notice the IMTM right-hand pattern.

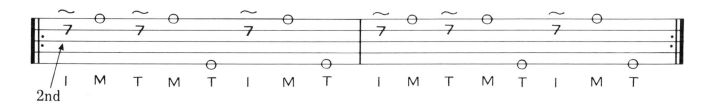

Exercise 4

The *chime* (△) is made by resting your index finger *gently* on top of the first 4 strings *right above* the 12th fret. See the photo below.

Experiment until you get just the right amount of pressure on the strings to make a chiming or bell-like sound.

Harmonics.

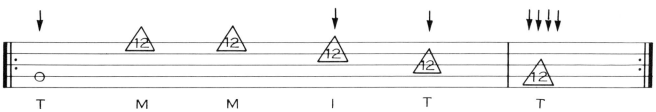

This sign (∼ . . . .) means to hold the choke (don't let it back down) for the length of the dotted line.

Lonesome Reuben

Traditional

D Tuning

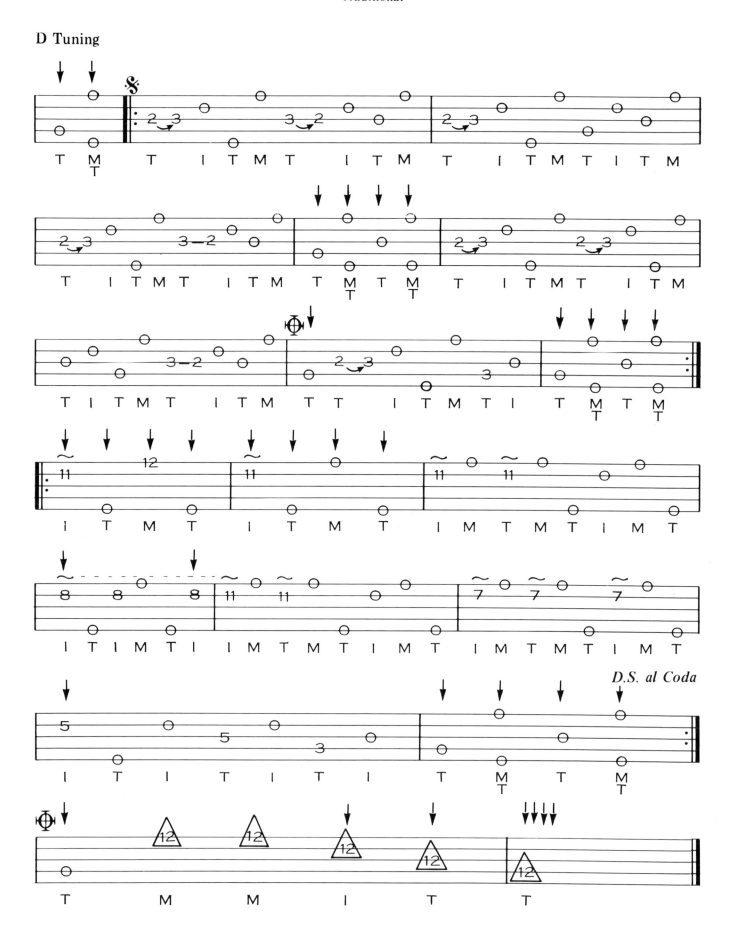

Lesson 29

Exercise 1

Here is a rather long slide which must be done
quickly.

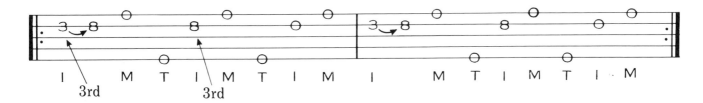

Exercise 2

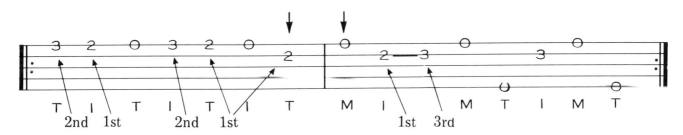

Exercise 3

The rhythm on the slide is identical to the slide
found in "Smoky Mountain Breakdown."

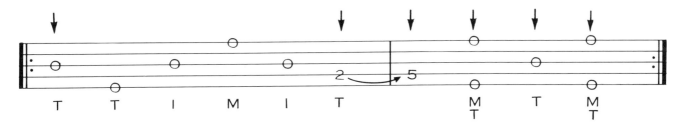

Exercise 4

Ending No. 1.

Here's a good all-purpose ending for almost
any song.

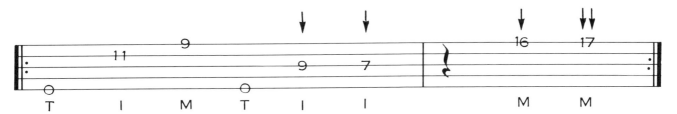

Union County Breakdown

D. Wayne Goforth

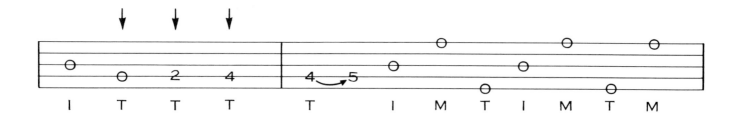

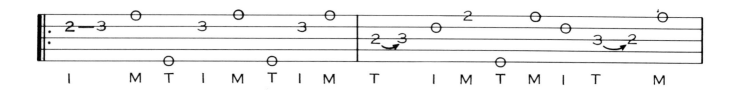

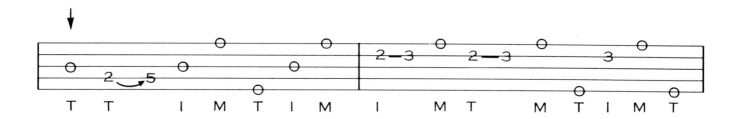

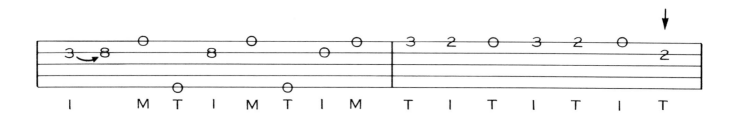

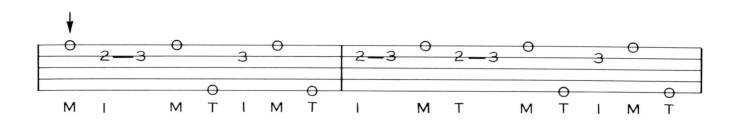

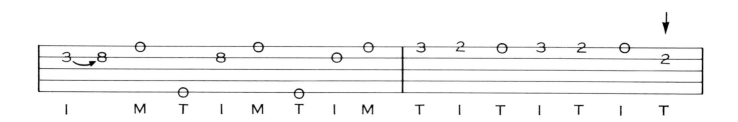

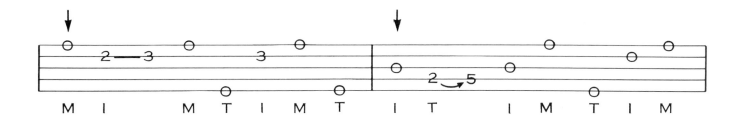

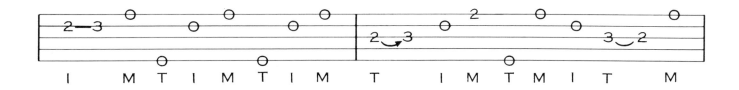

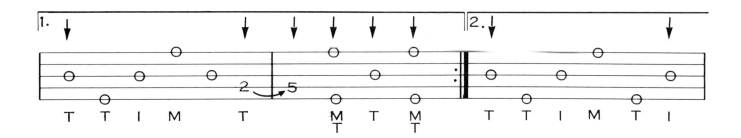

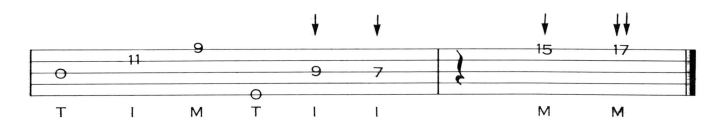

Lesson 30

Well, you're almost through! Try to find a friend
you can pick with.

Exercise 1

Sounds familiar?

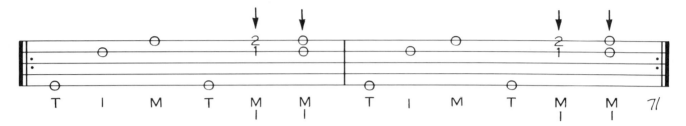

Exercise 2

Watch your timing on this one.

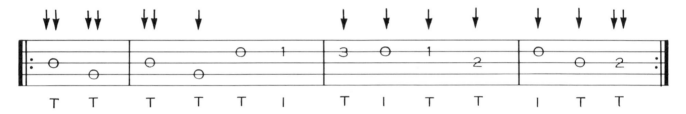

Exercise 3

Same here.

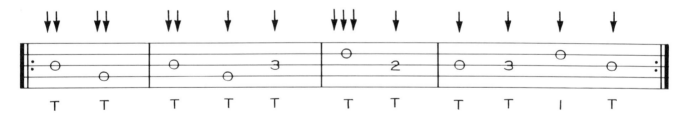

Exercise 4

This is simply a transition from a C to a G
Chord. Use 2nd finger.

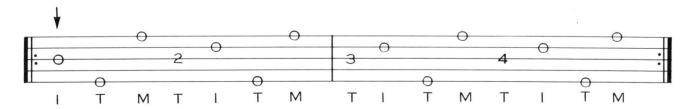

Remember, this is a duet between you and the guitar. This is why there are so many rests in the first part of the song.

𝄽 = one beat of silence.

▬ = two beats of silence.

▬ 𝄽 = three beats of silence.

▬ = four beats (or a full measure) of silence.

Feuding Banjos (Part 1)

D. Wayne Goforth

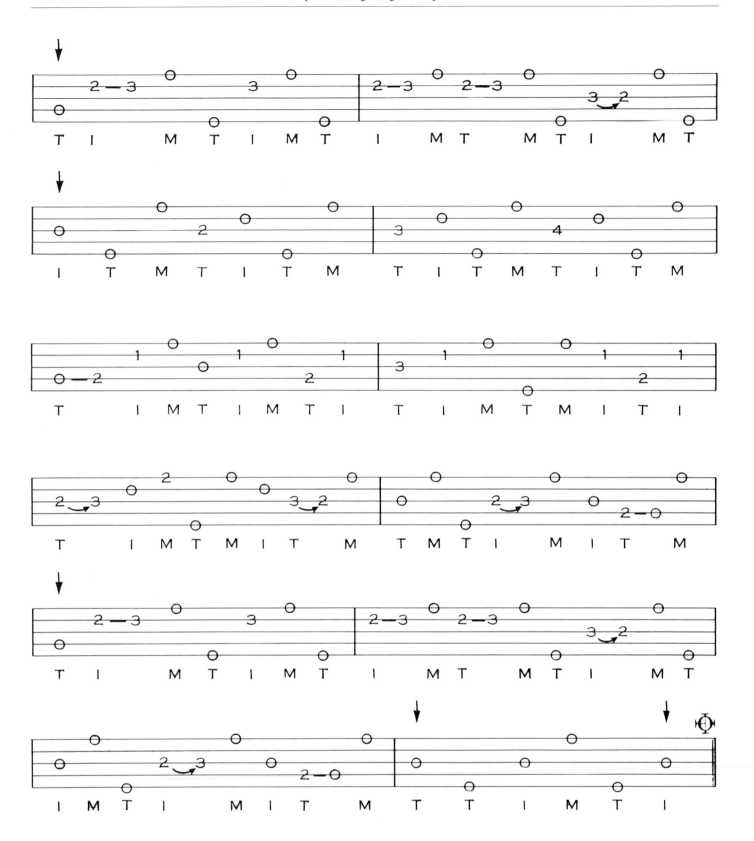

Continue with Lesson 31 before
playing the 2nd part of this song.

Lesson 31

These three exercises are basically the same,
but they occur at different positions on the neck.

Exercise 1

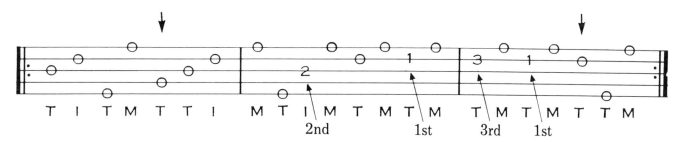

Exercise 2

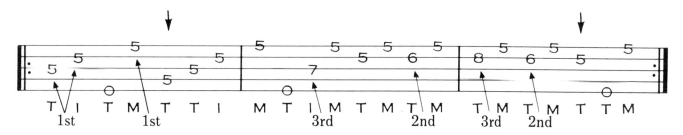

Exercise 3

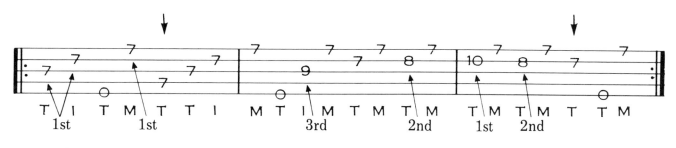

Exercise 4

Ending No. 2

Now, here's a new ending for you. Remember,
many endings are interchangeable. Use the
ones that *you* like.

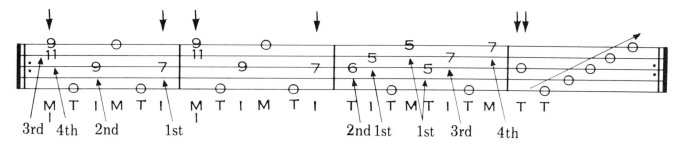

Feuding Banjos (Part 2)

Actually, in this song, the last 10 measures are considered to be *the ending.*

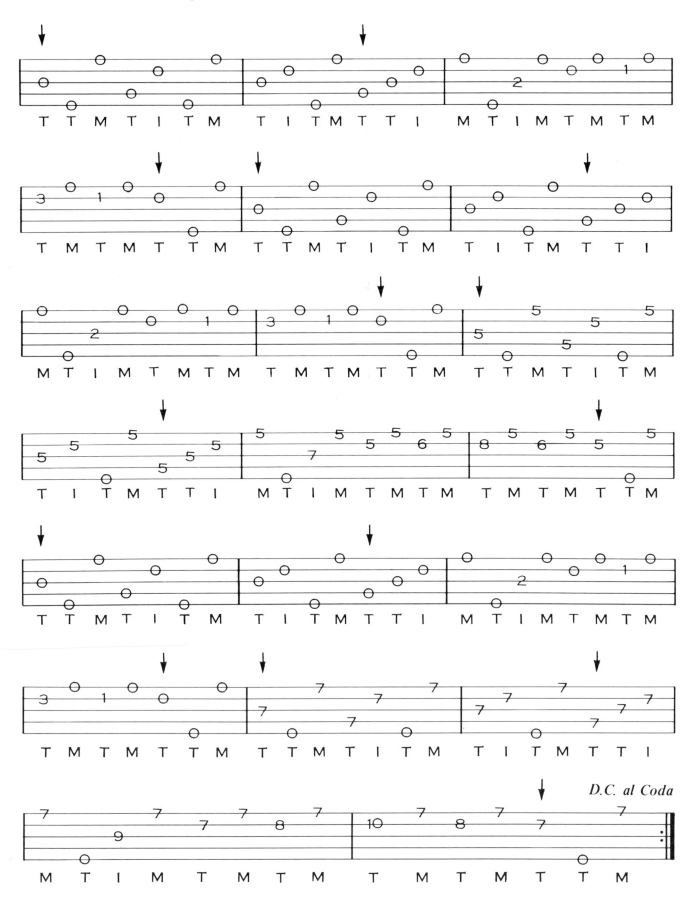

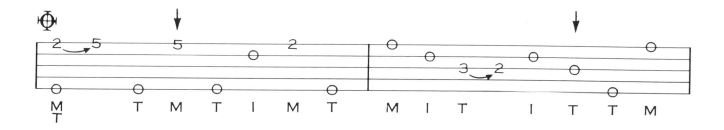

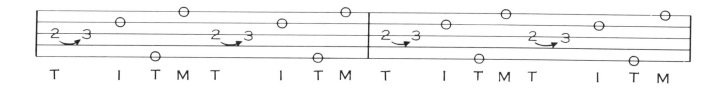

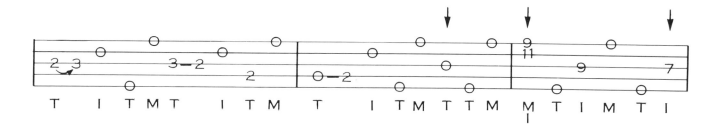

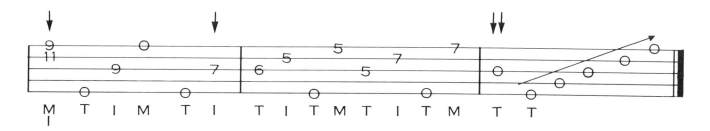

Lesson 32

Exercise 1

Watch your arrows and left-hand fingering here.

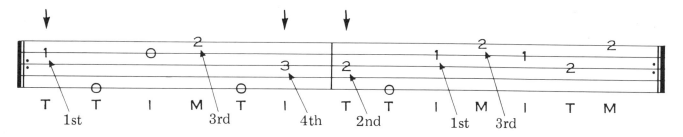

Exercise 2

Same here . . .

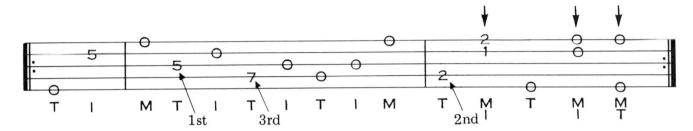

Exercise 3

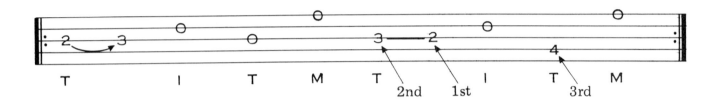

Exercise 4

Ending No. 3

Remember, most endings are interchangeable.

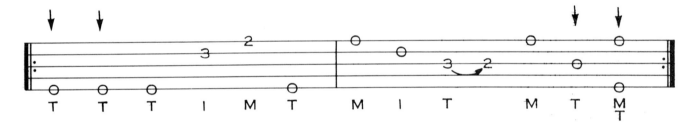

The Forty-Niner

D. Wayne Goforth

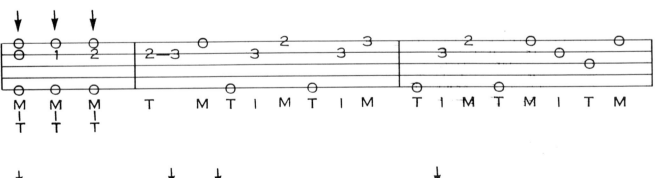

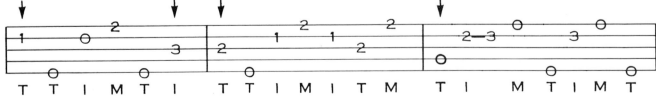

Lesson 33

Here is a good example of the chromatic style of picking *combined* with the straight-out bluegrass style. Remember to listen and learn to recognize the various chromatic patterns. Most of them are pretty standard and reoccur in many banjo tunes. Pay particular attention to your *left-hand fingering* on all chromatic runs. If there is a secret to chromatic style, this is it.

Exercise 1

Here is an *inside roll* (on the inside strings).

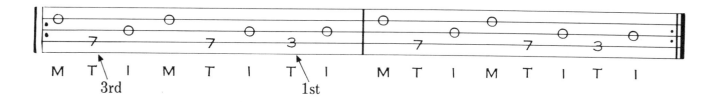

Exercise 2

Left-hand position remains the same in
measures 2 and 3.

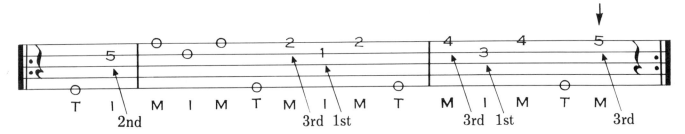

Exercise 3

Ending No. 4

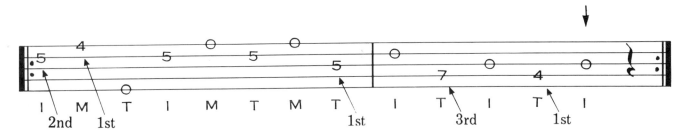

Exercise 4

Here's a chromatic ending for you.

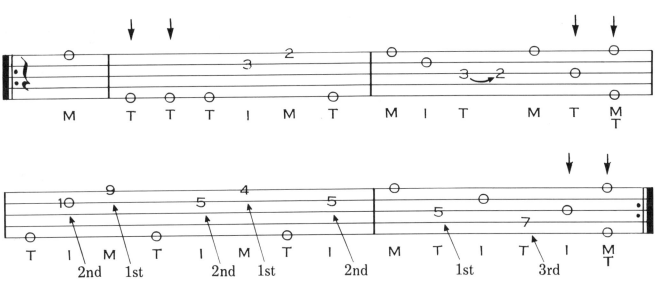

Bill Cheatham

Traditional

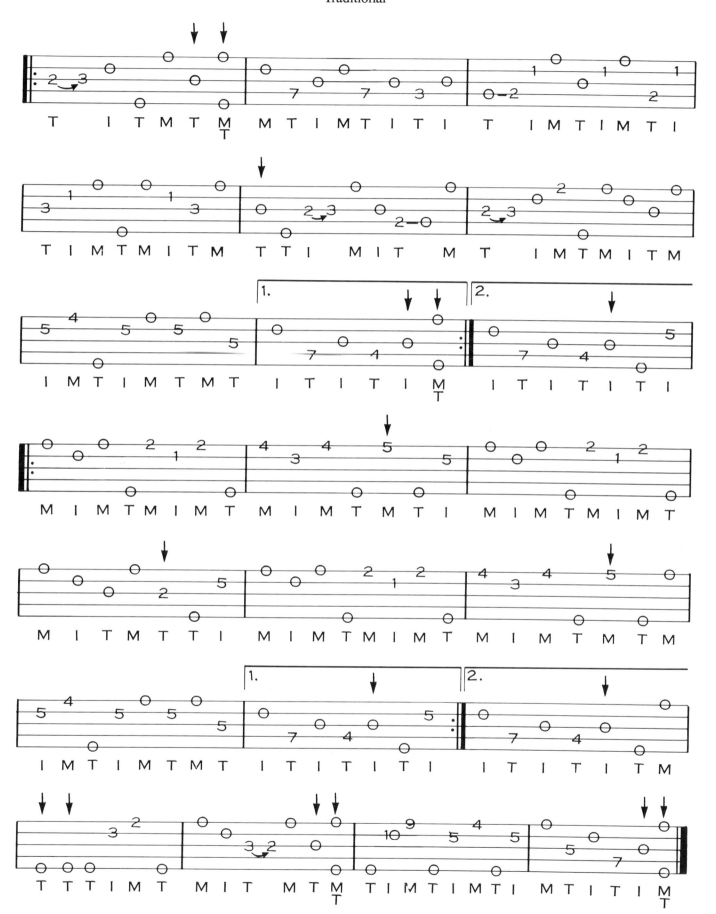

Lesson 34

Exercise 1

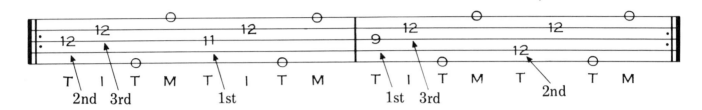

Exercise 2

Notice the similarity between this exercise and the previous one. Play them together, in sequence, after you've mastered them.

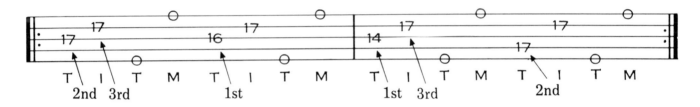

Exercise 3

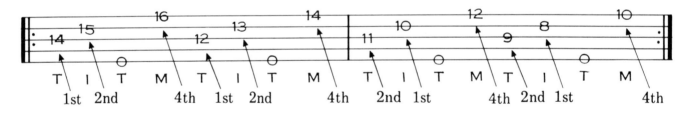

Exercise 4

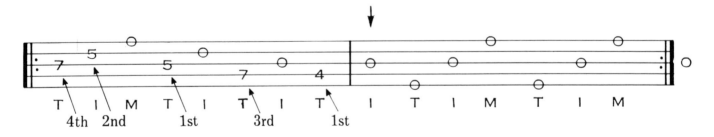

Exercise 5

Ending No. 5

This ending is a little tricky, but well worth learning. The notes in brackets are to be played each as *one* beat – that is, *three* notes in the time it usually takes to play *one*. This is called a *triplet* and is counted like this:

Main Count:

One   two   three   four   one

Triple Count:

One   one-two-three   one-two-three   one-two-three

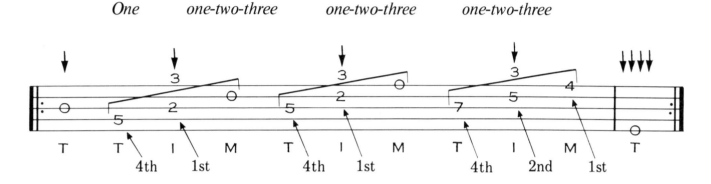

Toby's Mountain

D. Wayne Goforth

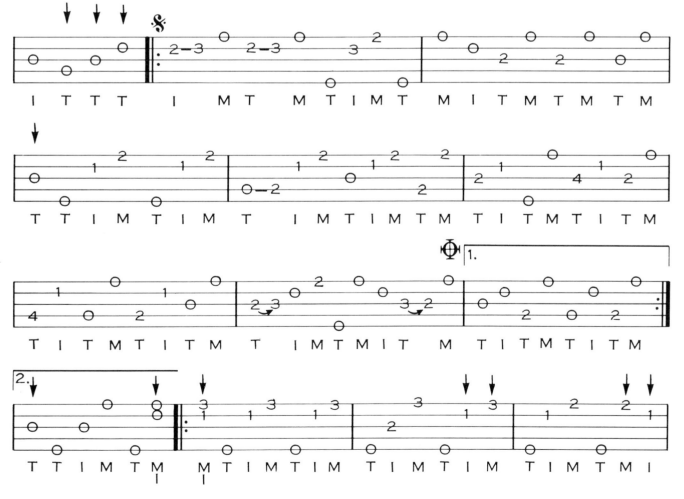

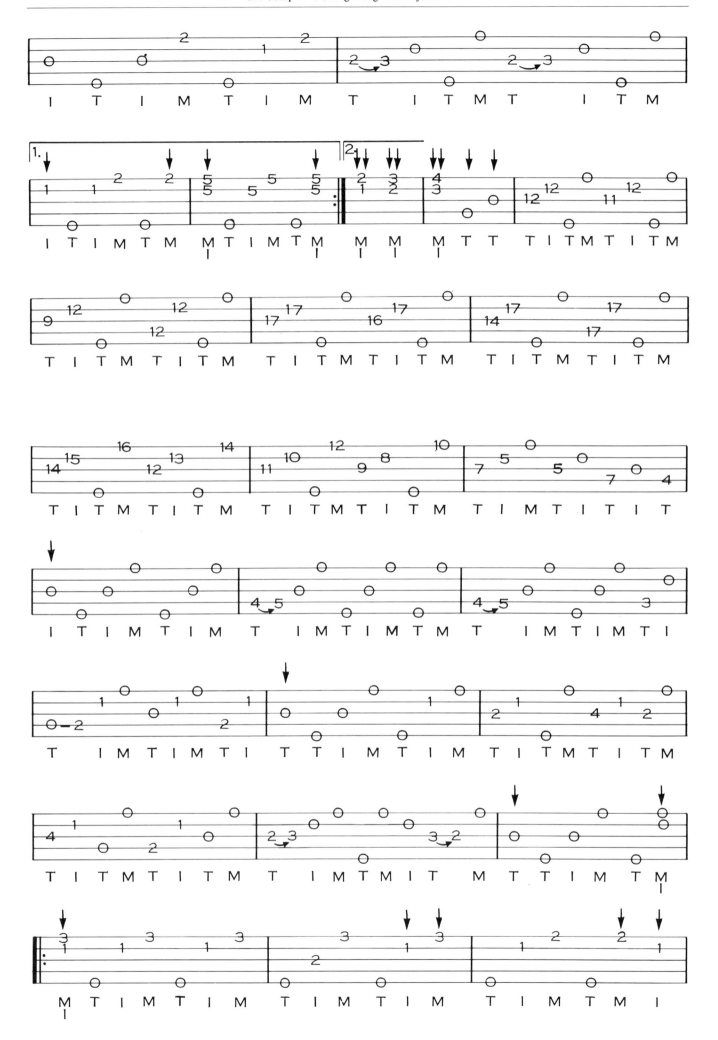

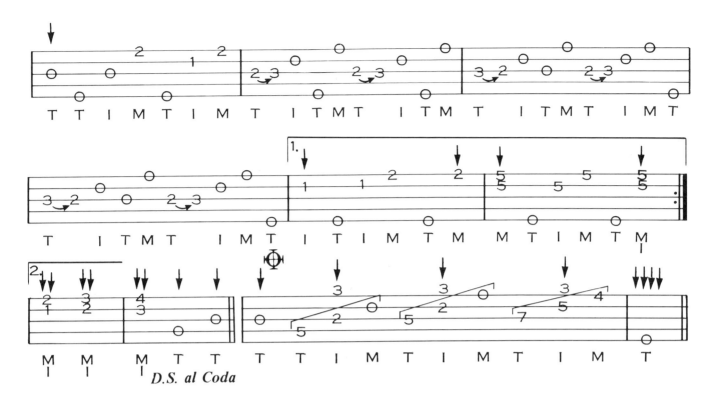

Lesson 35

Exercise 1

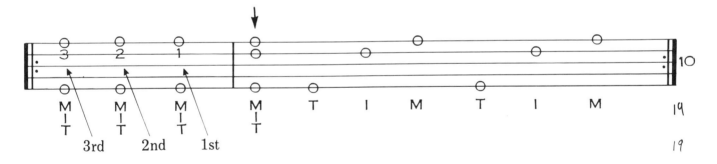

Exercise 2

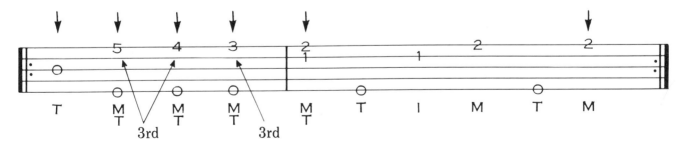

Exercise 3

Two notes tied together like this 1 ⤵ 1 indicates a *tie*. The notes should be sustained over into the next measure.

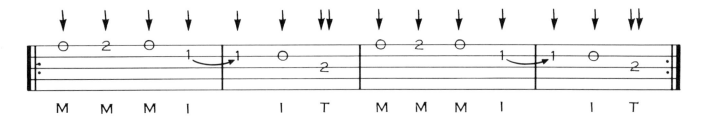

Exercise 4

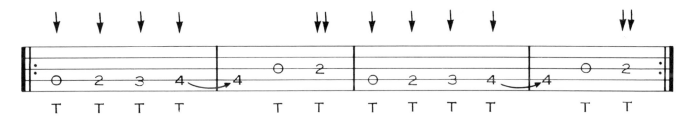

Down Yonder

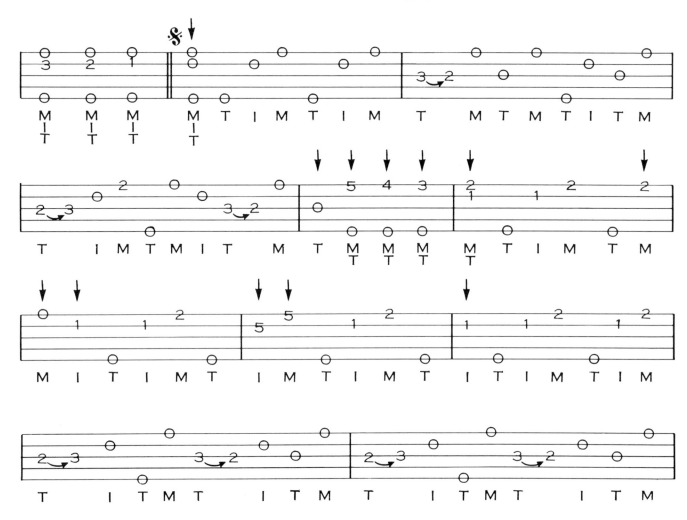

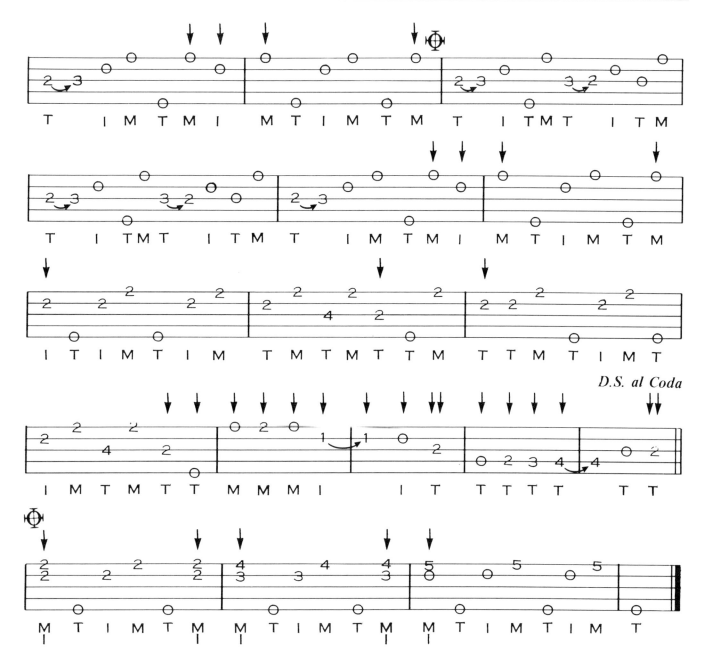

Lesson 36

Whenever you see two adjacent strings with the same fret number (as below), it is a pretty safe bet that you can *barre* these notes with one finger. Usually, you use the 1st finger of your left hand to barre.

Exercise 1

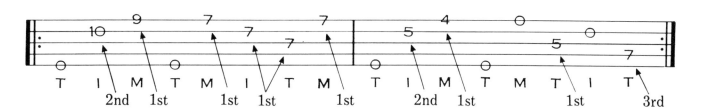

Exercise 2

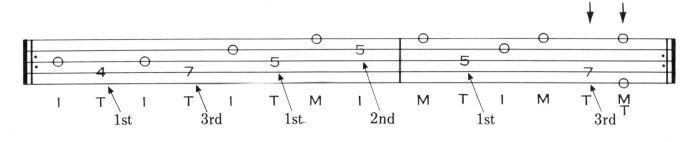

Exercise 3

Watch your timing here. Count the rhythm out
in your head before you play it.

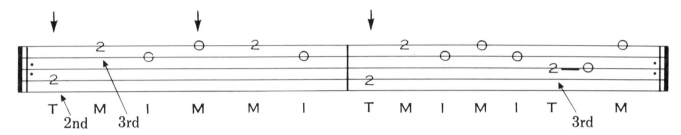

Exercise 4

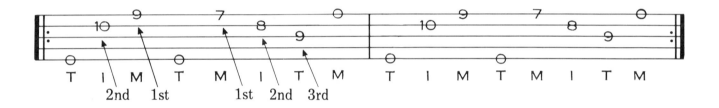

Blackberry Blossom

Traditional

This song is almost all chromatic style.

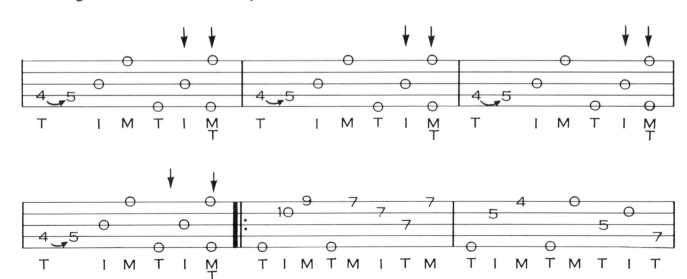

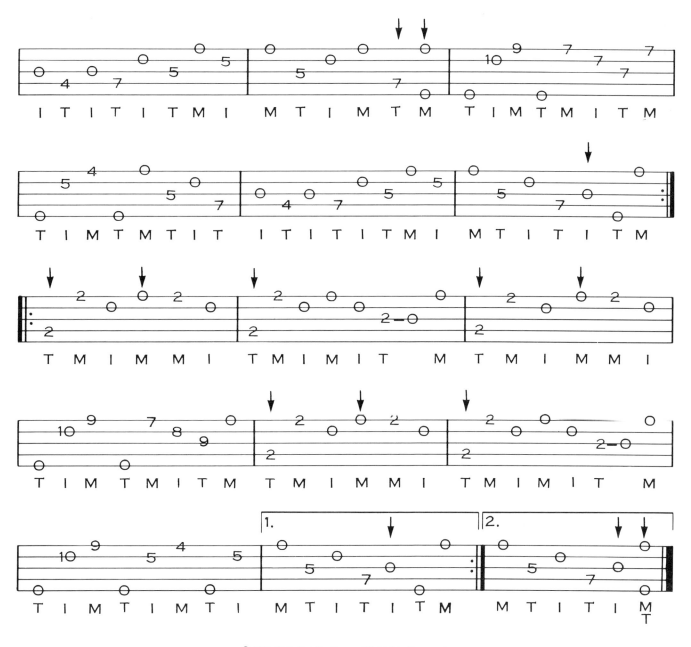

Lesson 37

Exercise 1

Here's one where you can really show off. Use
your 1st finger for the pull-off.

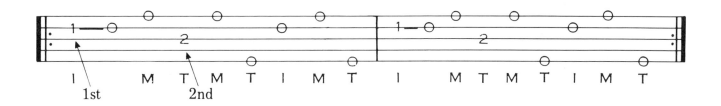

The next two exercises are almost identical except for their starting positions on the neck. Practice them as one exercise after you've learned them.

Exercise 2A

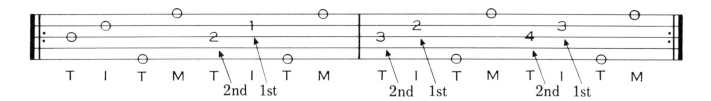

Exercise 2B

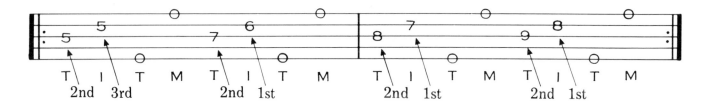

These three exercises are also similar. Master each one individually and then practice them slowly, in sequence, gradually increasing your speed.

Exercise 3A

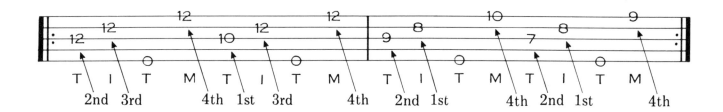

Exercise 3B

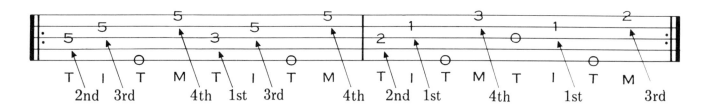

Exercise 3C

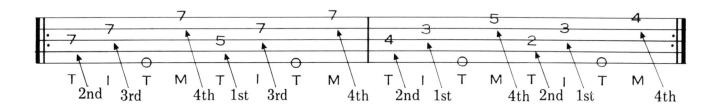

Dixie Daybreak

D. Wayne Goforth

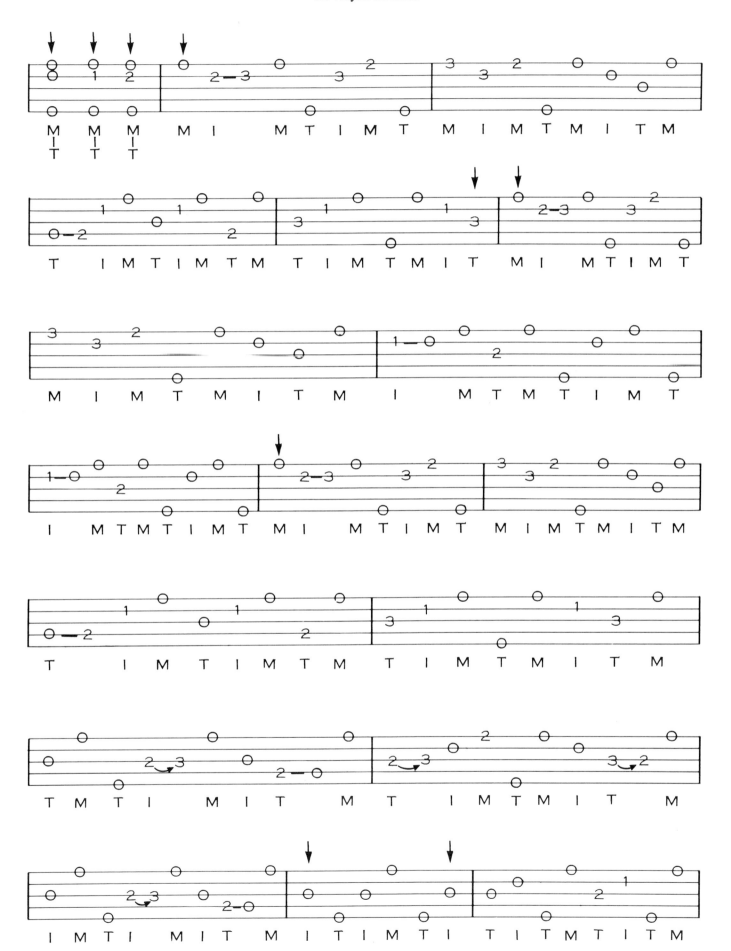

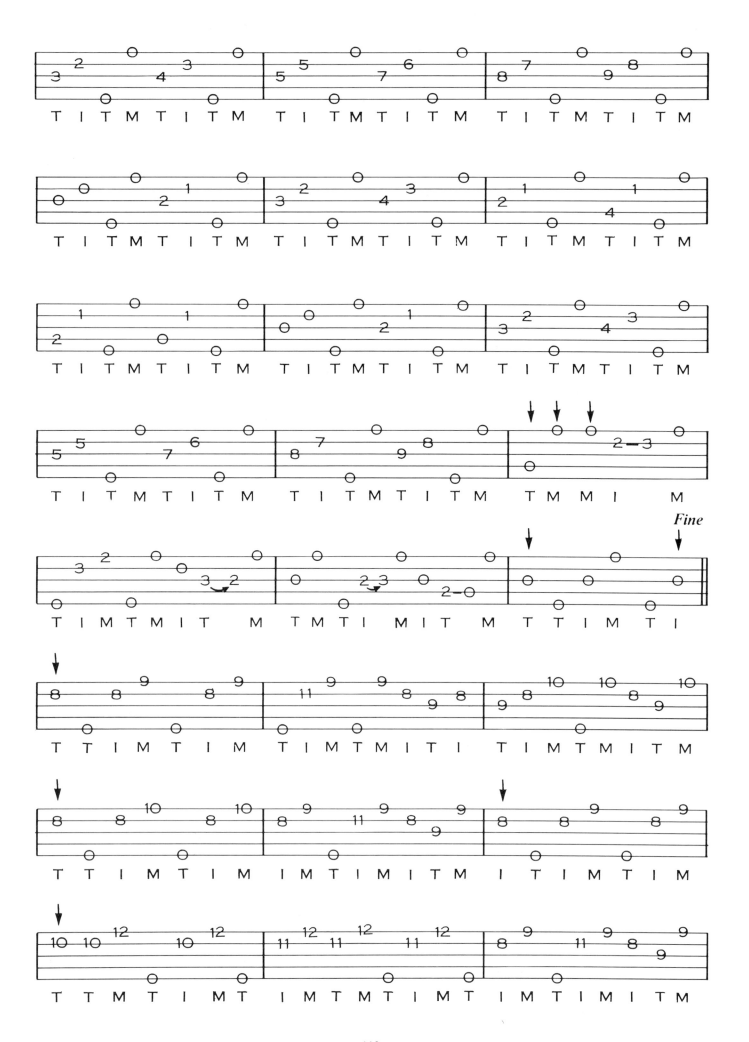

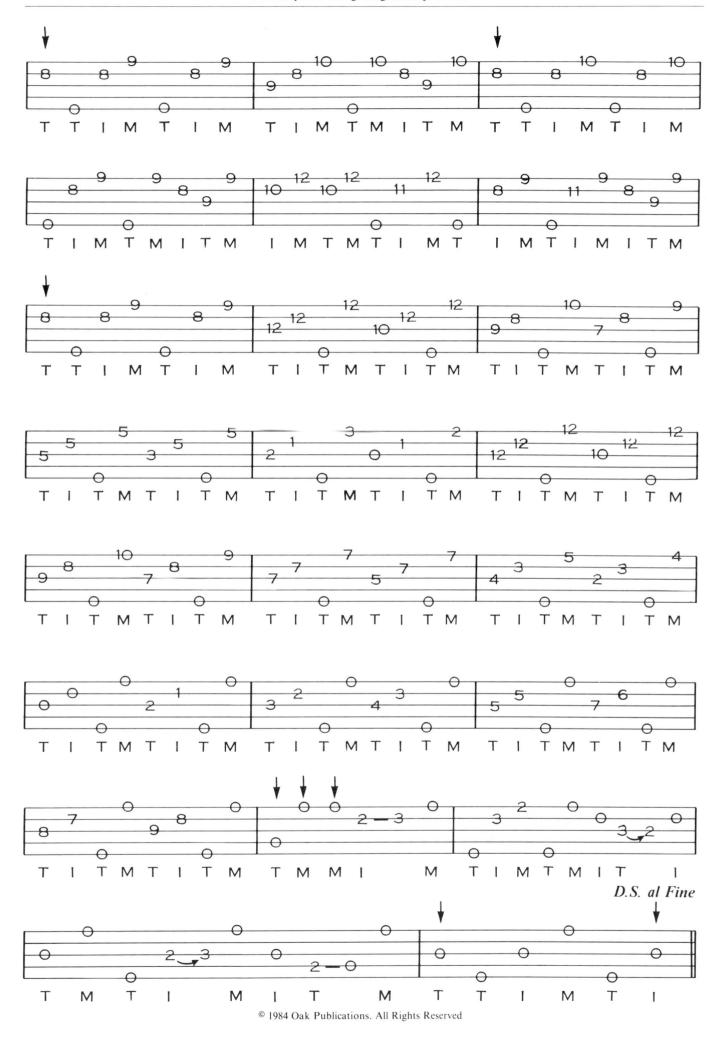

Lesson 38

Exercise 1

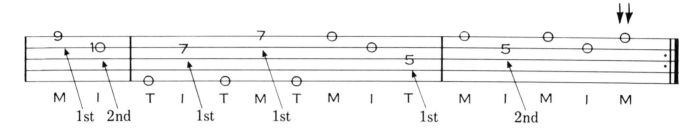

Exercise 2

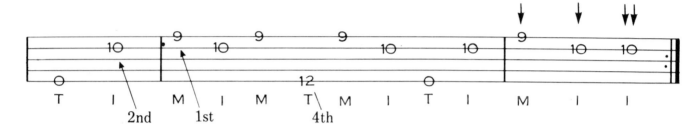

Exercise 3A

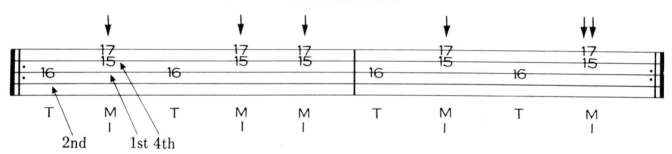

Exercise 3B

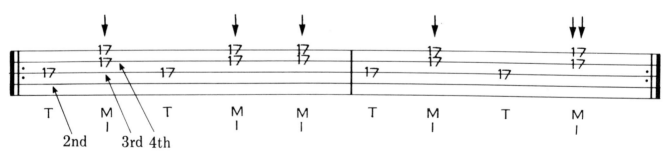

Exercise 4

This exercise is the same as the previous one
except for a fingering and fret change.

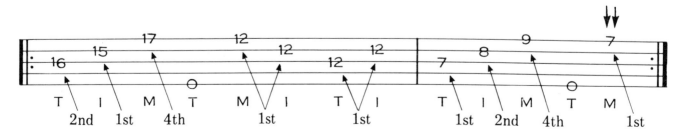

Turkey In The Straw

Traditional

Here is a chromatic style arrangement of an old favorite. (Be sure to watch your left-hand fingering.)

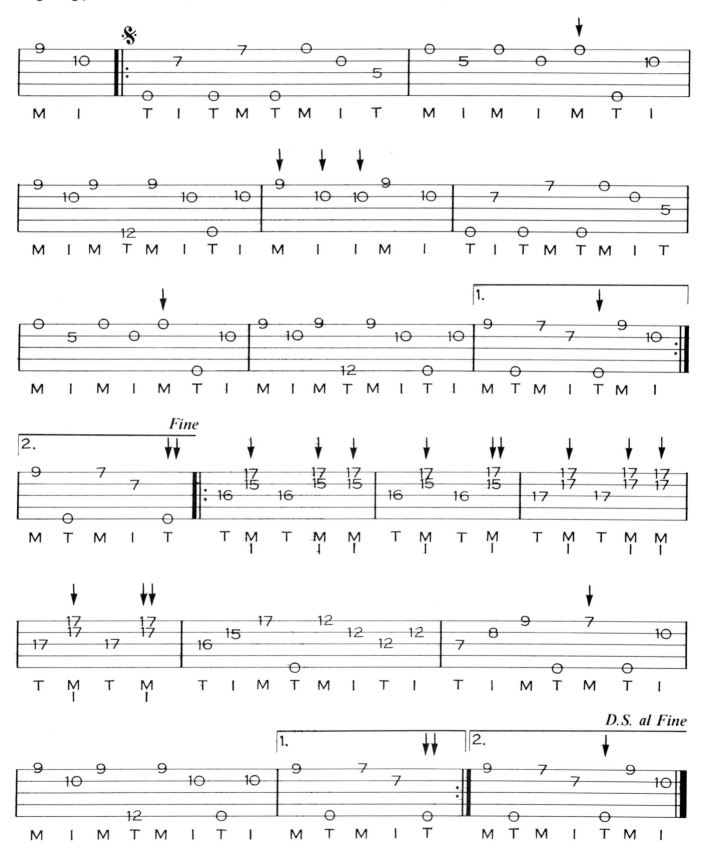

Lesson 39

The next two exercises change from one chord
to another.

Exercise 1

G to B7 . . .

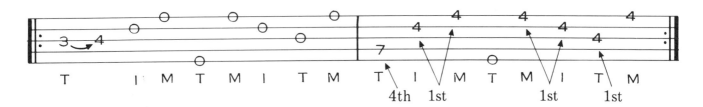

Exercise 2

D to D Augmented . . .

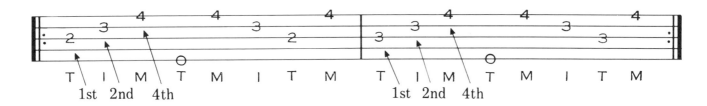

Exercise 3

Note how the 1st and 3rd fingers move up the
fretboard together.

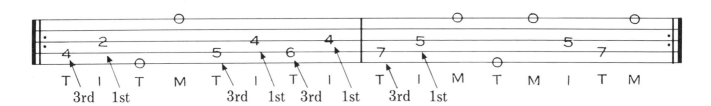

Exercise 4

Here is a nice D run you can use in many songs
in the key of G, once they reach the *turnaround*
(the end-part of the song just before you start
over again).

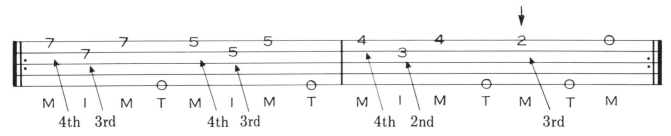

The Old Farm Place

D. Wayne Goforth

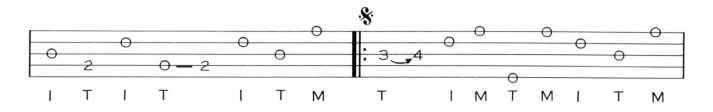

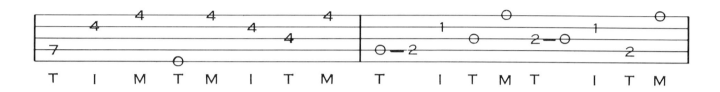

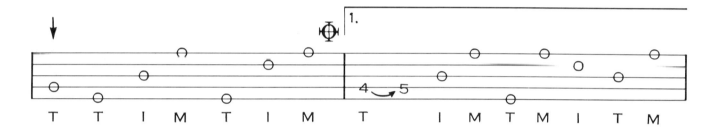

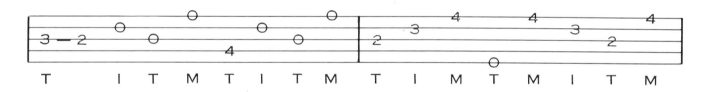

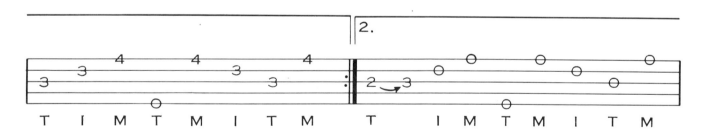

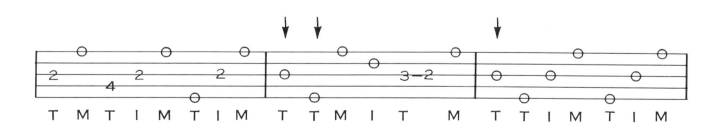

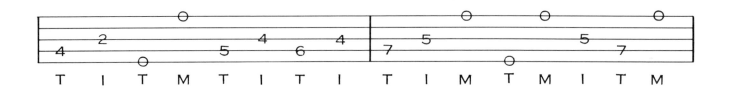

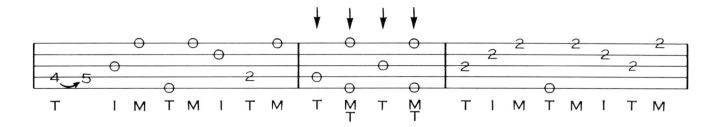

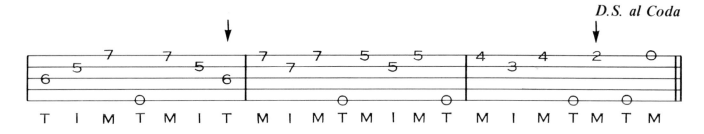

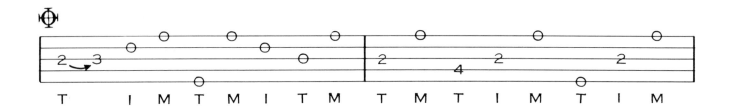

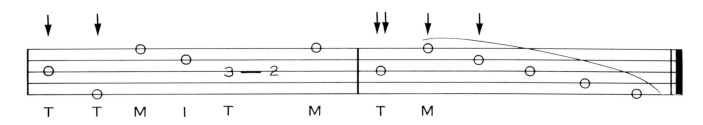

Lesson 40

Exercise 1

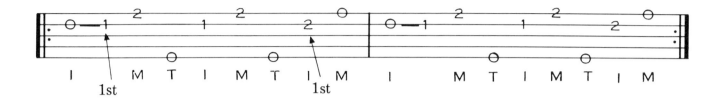

Are you *memorizing* the patterns as you go along?

Exercise 2

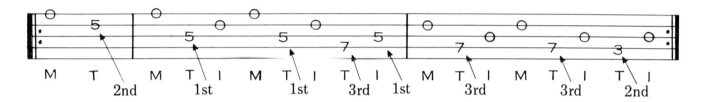

Exercise 3

Watch your rhythm here.

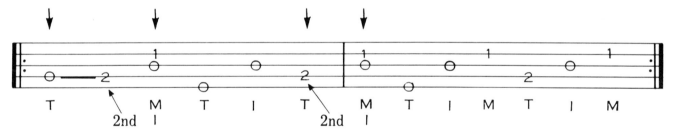

Shenandoah Daybreak (Part 1)

D. Wayne Goforth

Here is another showy tune combining the best of straight bluegrass and chromatic styles.

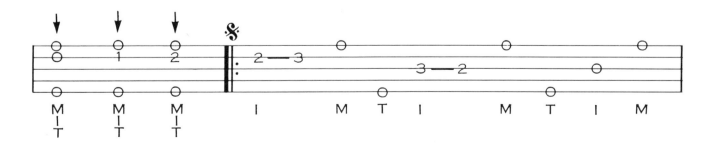

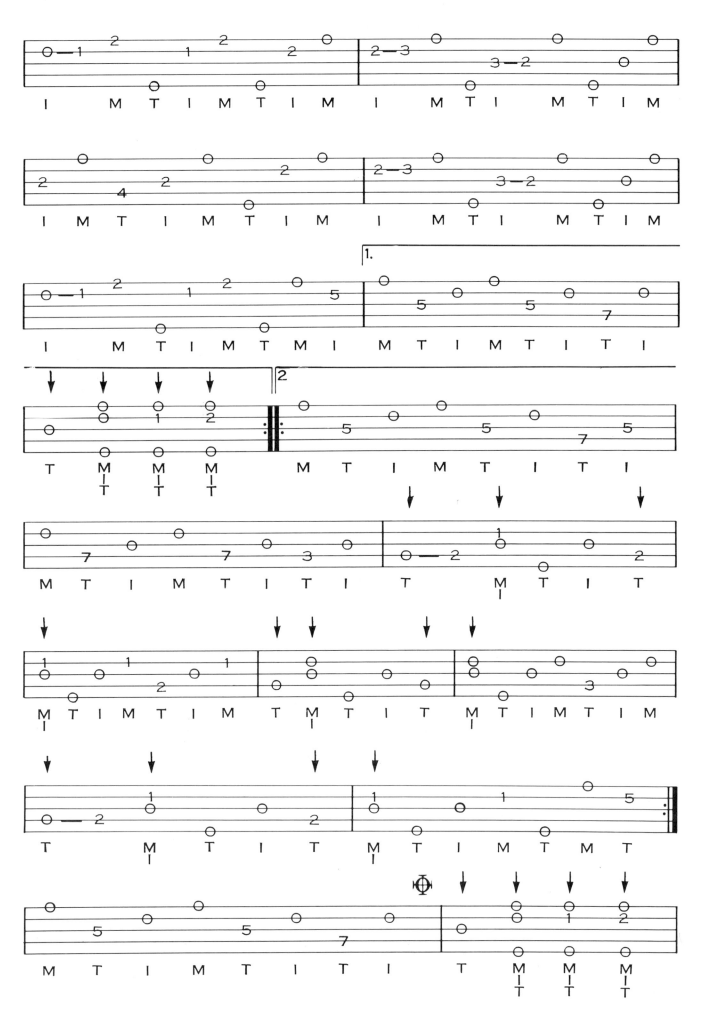

Continue with Lesson 41 before
playing the 2nd part of this song.

Lesson 41

Exercise 1

Remember the importance of correct left-hand fingering.

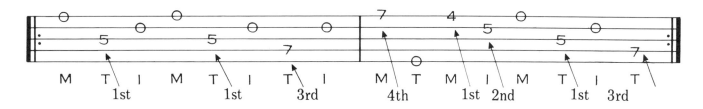

Exercise 2

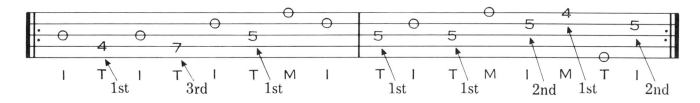

Exercise 3

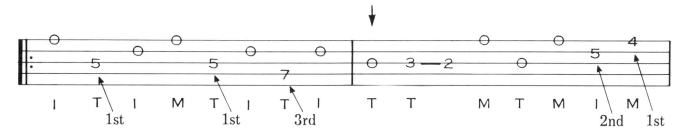

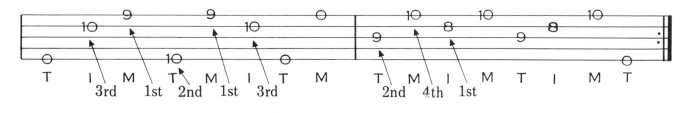

Exercise 4

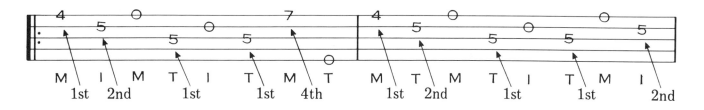

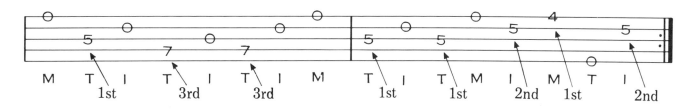

Shenandoah Daybreak (Part 2)

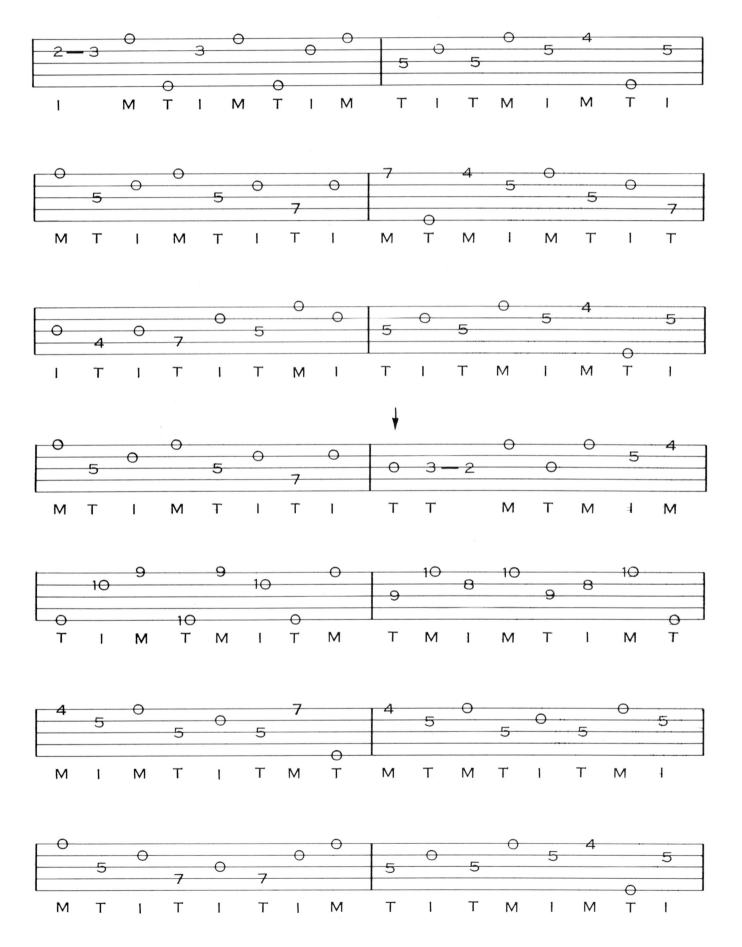

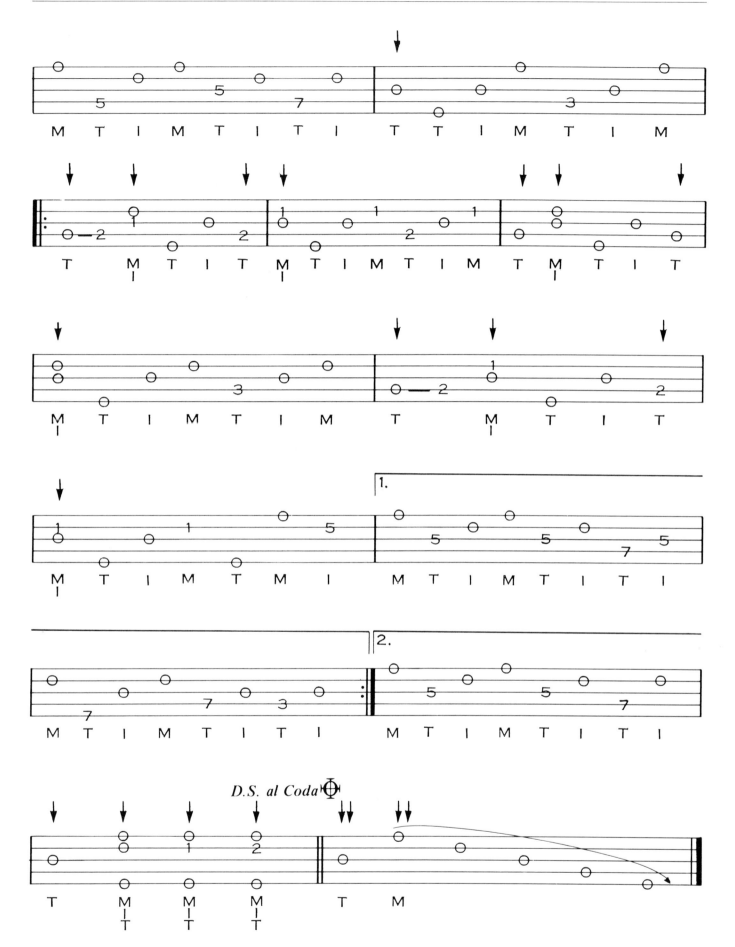

Lesson 42

Exercise 1

Review the explanation of the triplet in
Lesson 4.

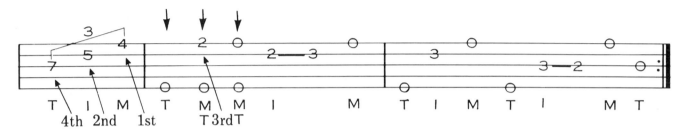

Exercise 2

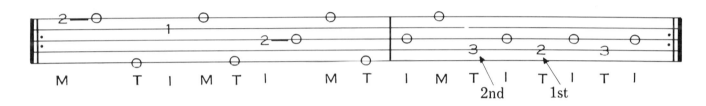

Exercise 3

Watch your time here!

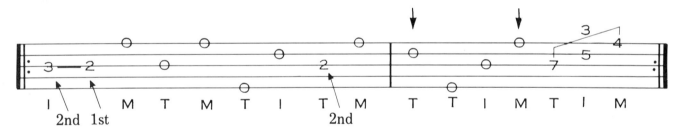

Arab Bounce

Jimmy Martin & Vernon Derrick

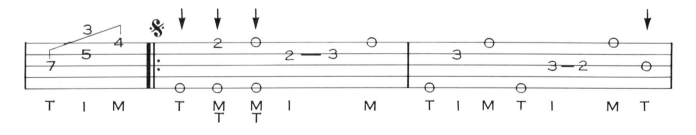

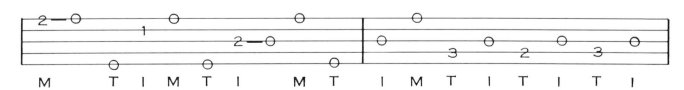

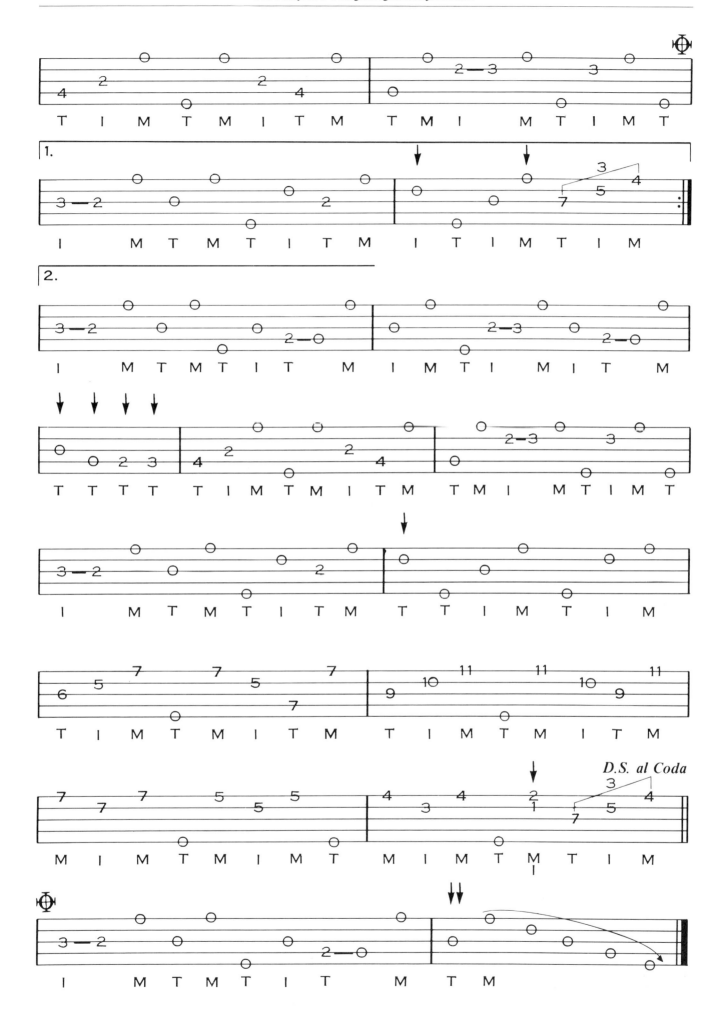

Lesson 43

Chromatic style picking is sometimes referred to as "Hornpiping". This style was played by sailors in Old England on pipes made of horn.

Many of the sea shanties, Irish jigs, etc. from this period have chromatic melodies.

Exercise 1

Be sure to use the suggested fingering on frets 9 and 10. Barre 7th fret with your 1st finger in the 2nd measure.

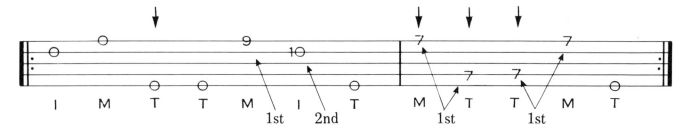

Exercise 2

Begin this exercise with a D chord, then go into your hornpiping fingering.

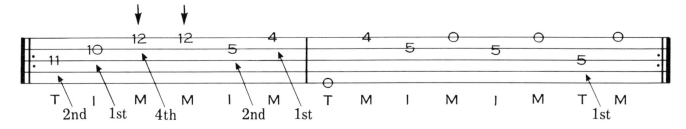

Exercise 3

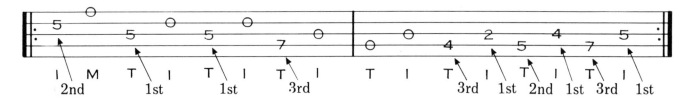

Exercise 4

Start on an A chord and move that same left-hand position up to the 10th fret to form your D chord.

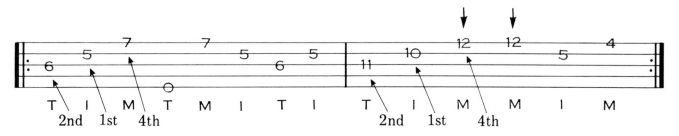

Exercise 5

Ending No. 6

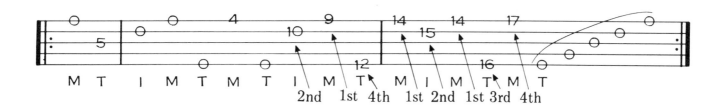

Sailor's Hornpipe

Traditional

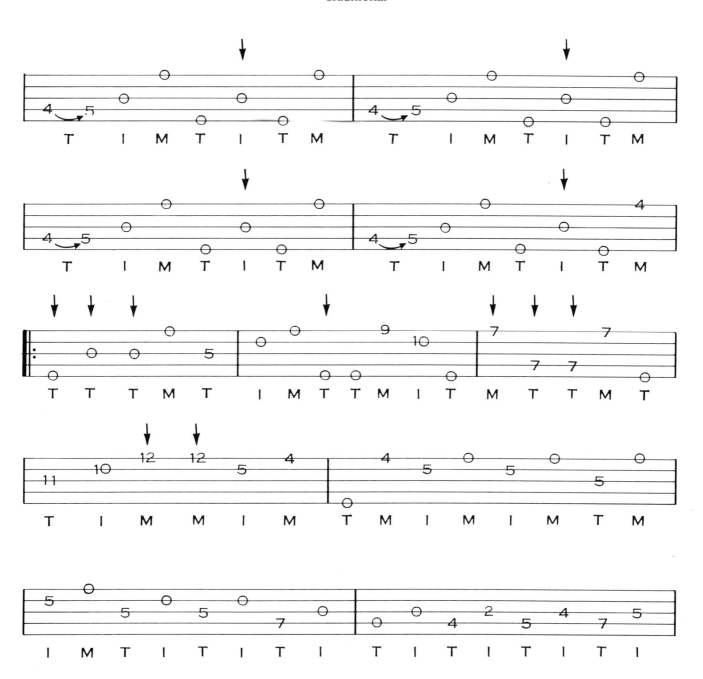

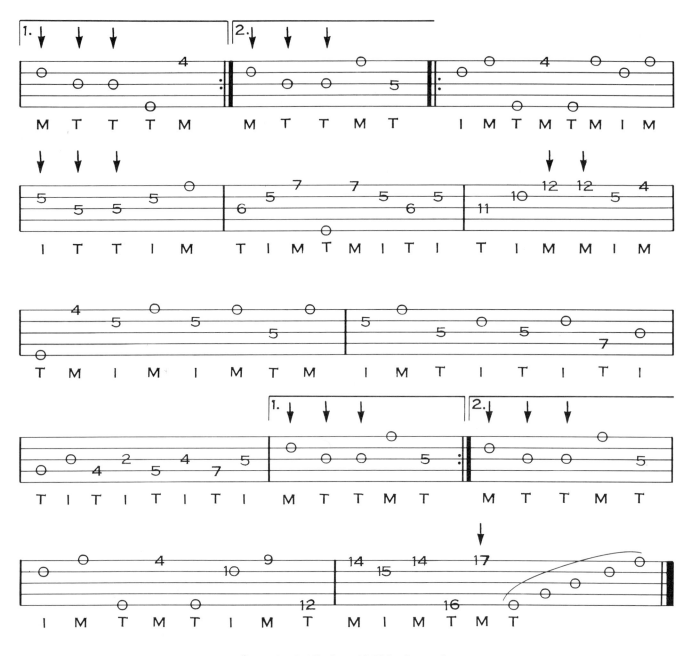

Lesson 44

Exercise 1

Be sure to watch your left-hand fingering here.
This is a common pattern easily worked into
many songs.

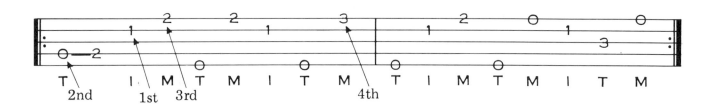

Exercise 2

B chord at the 4th fret. Simply barre with your
1st finger.

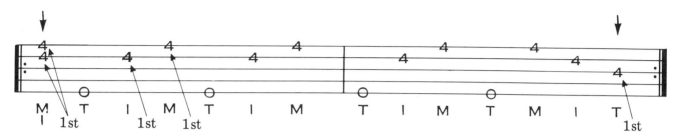

Exercise 3

This exercise is built around an E major chord.

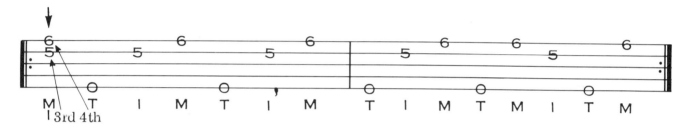

Exercise 4

And this one around an A major chord.

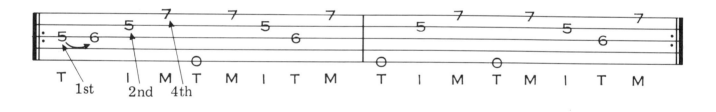

Exercise 5

Ending No. 7

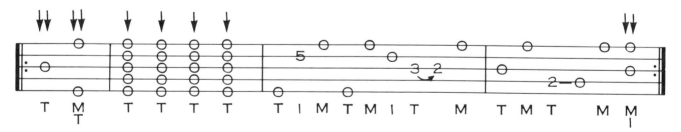

Lesson 45

Exercise 1

Watch your timing on this first exercise. Count
out loud if it helps.

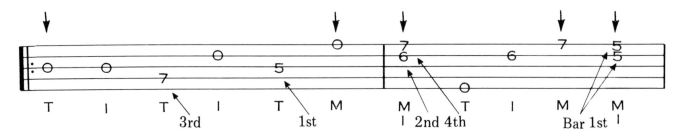

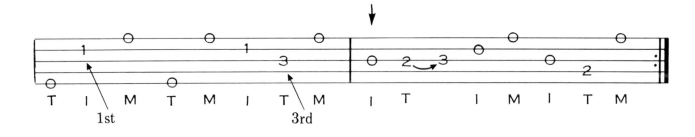

Exercise 2

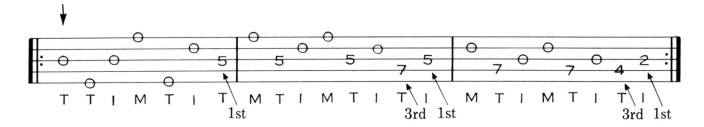

Exercise 3

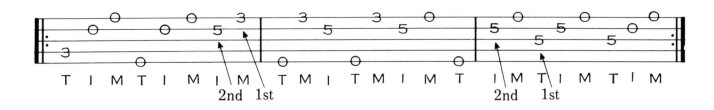

Exercise 4

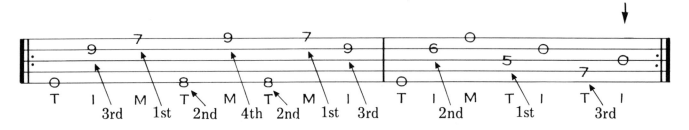

Foxfire

Garland Shuping

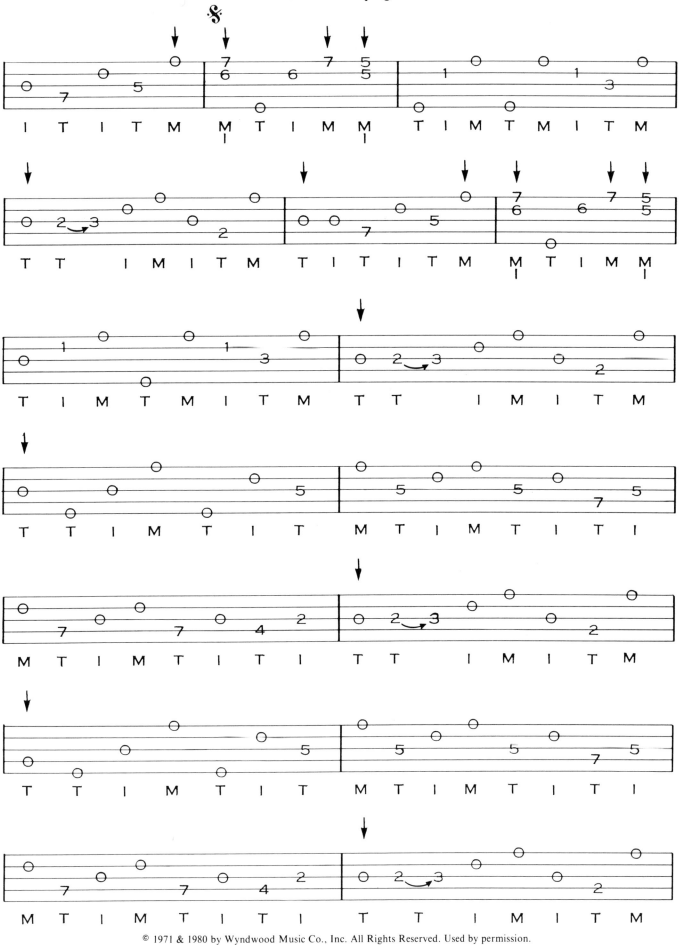

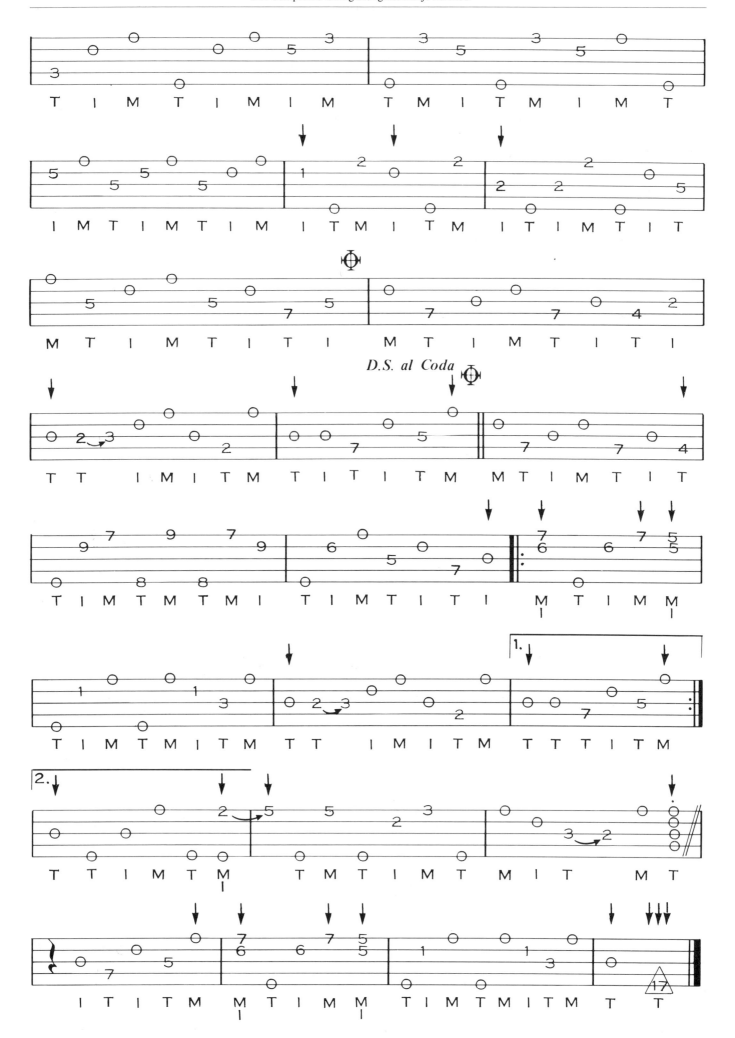

Lesson 46

Exercise 1

Remember this C7 chord at the 8th fret?

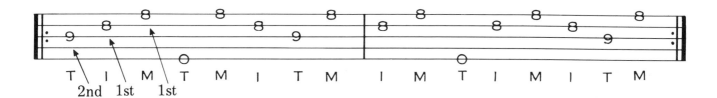

Exercise 2

Be sure to alternate *thumb* and *index* in measure 3.

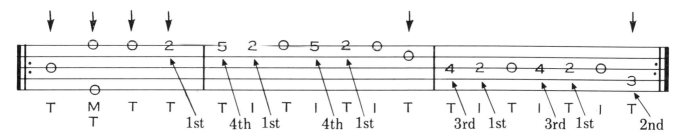

Exercise 3

E chord at the 9th fret.

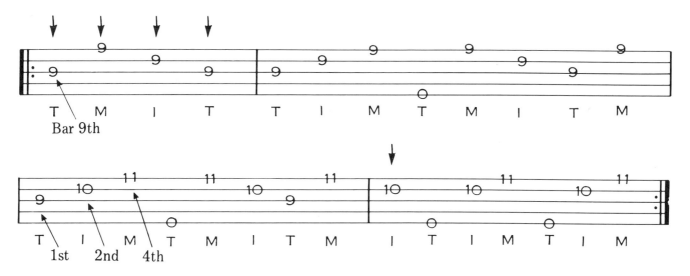

Exercise 4

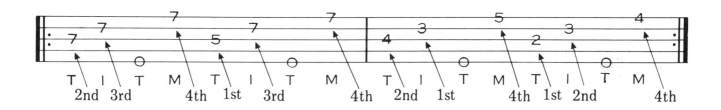

As you can see, most of the measures in this song are blank . . . this means it's been left up to *your* imagination. We have provided only the measures which will make this song distinctly "Hickory Creek".

Sooner or later you will have to learn the art of improvising a song. You know by now that there are certain rolls and licks which fit with the chord of G . . . certain ones for C, D7, A, etc. Recall the licks that you know and play the ones that will *fit* with the chords provided.

If you choose to write them in, pay attention to your timing. If you use 6 regular notes, you must have 1 arrowed note in that measure, 4 notes, 2 arrows, and so on. There are 4 *full* beats to a measure.

Hopefully, you will begin to go back now and improvise other songs you have learned, replacing instructed segments with ones *you* like better.

You may even want to try your hand at working up a song from scratch, picking out the melody and filling in around it with licks and rolls which you know.

Only through improvisation and the creation of your own arrangements will you reach full maturity as a banjo player. Be eager to learn from other banjo players, trade licks with them and such. You can never learn too much. It would also be a good idea to master the art of getting a song from a record and into your repertoire. This can be time consuming, but it is well worth the effort.

Using the techniques discussed above, your growth as a banjo player will depend totally upon yourself. The sky's the limit! So let's begin. This one's all yours.

Hickory Creek

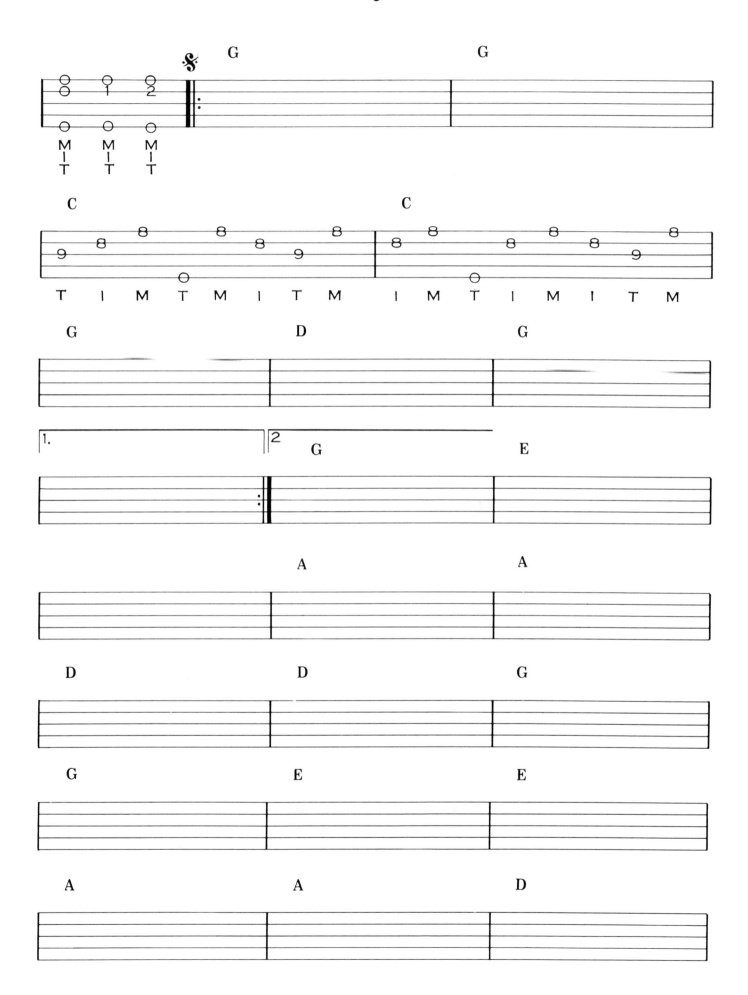

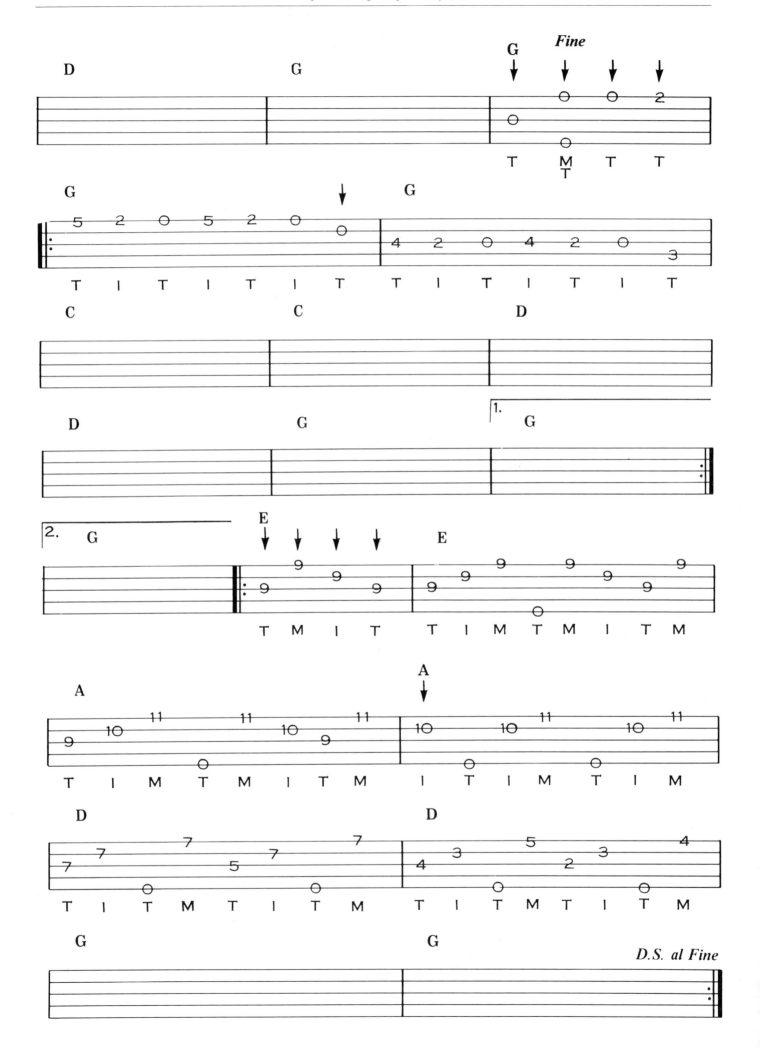

Lesson 47

By now you should have no problems with the exercises.

Exercise 1

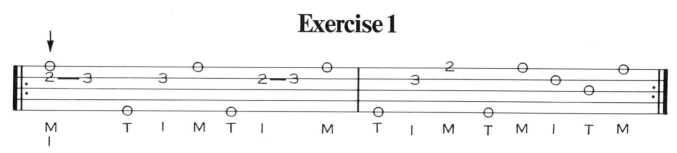

Exercise 2

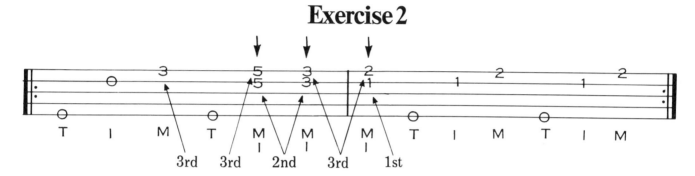

Exercise 3

Exercise 4

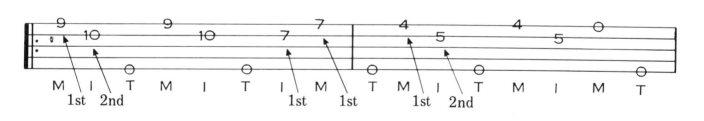

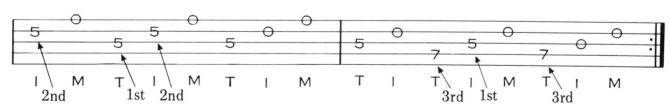

Exercise 5

L'il Dave (Part 1)

On this tune by Vic Jordan, be sure to have the correct left-hand fingering, and don't sacrifice accuracy for premature speed.

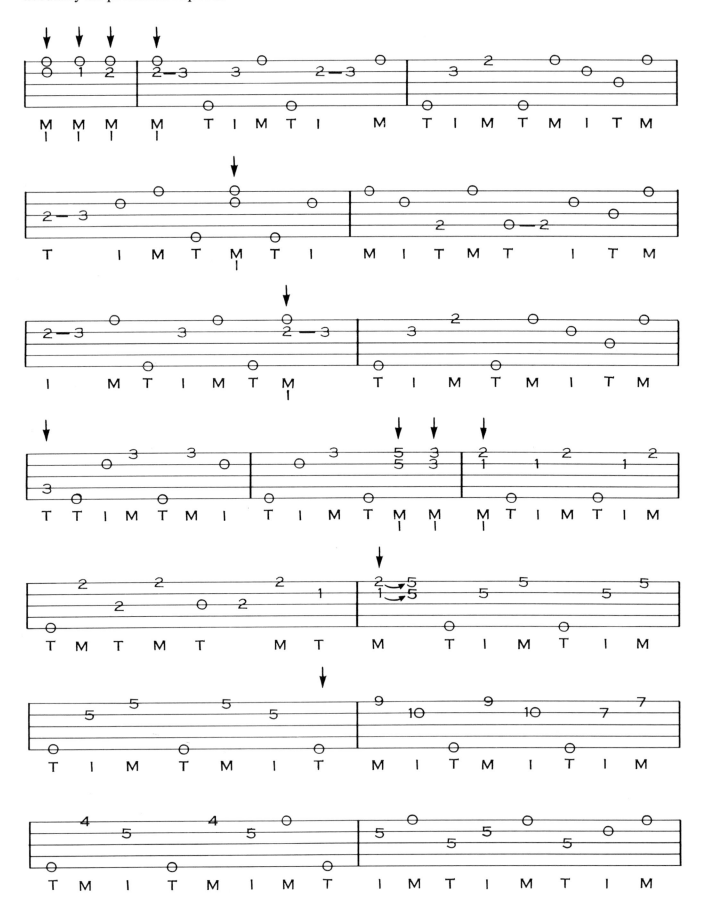

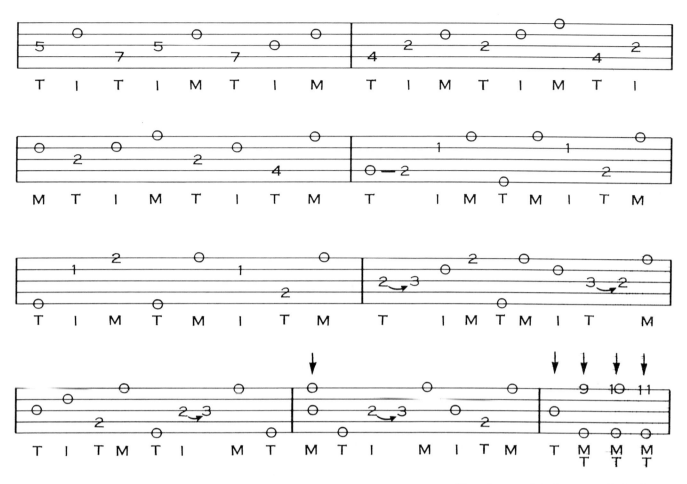

Continue with Lesson 48 before
playing the 2nd part of this song.

Lesson 48

Exercise 1

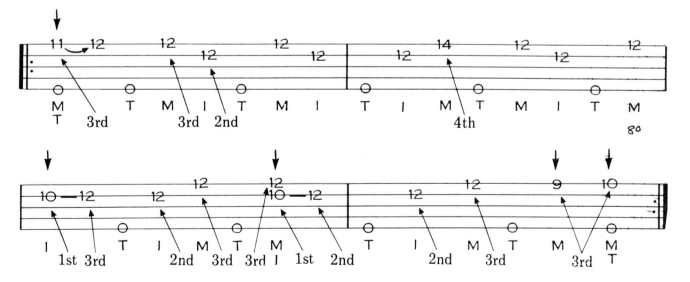

Exercise 2

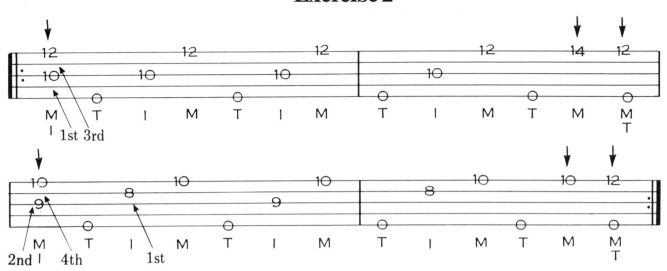

Exercise 3

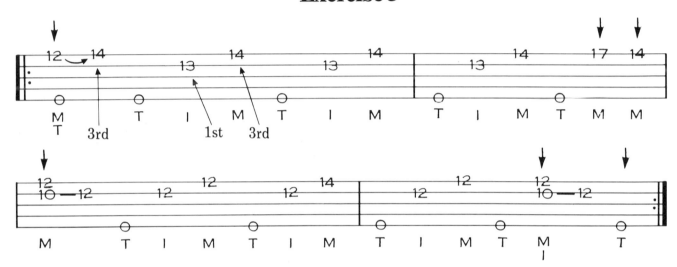

Exercise 4

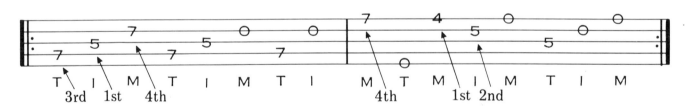

Exercise 5

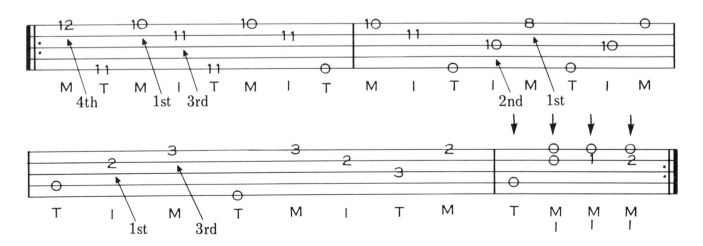

L'il Dave (Part 2)

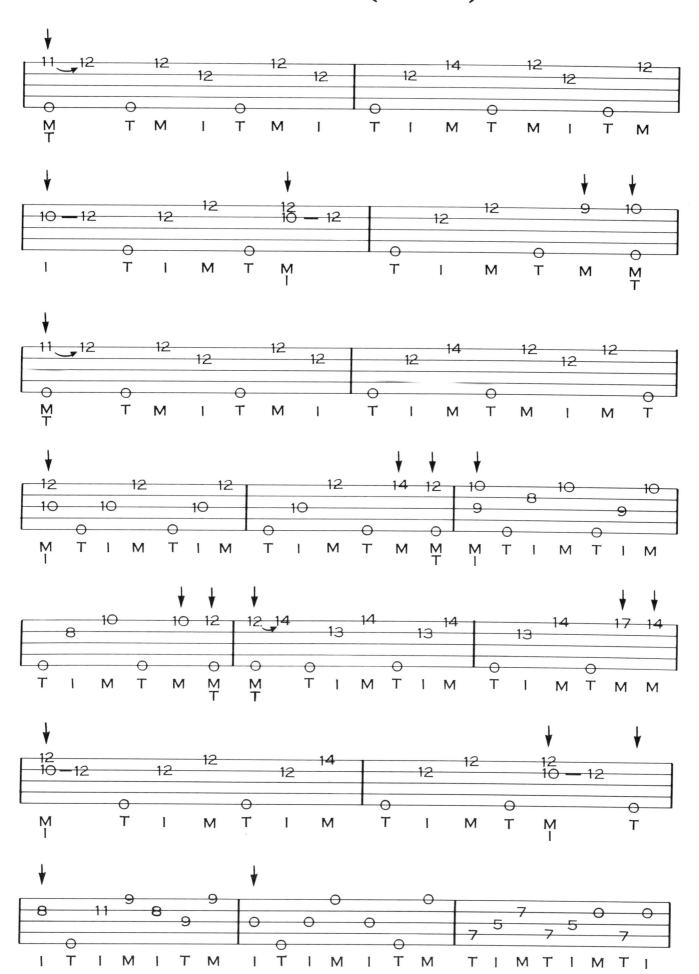

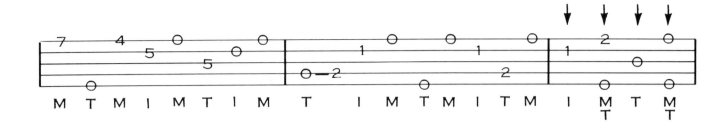

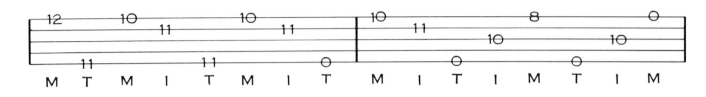

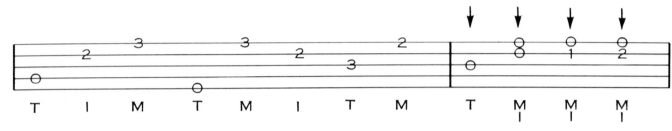

Continue with Lesson 49 before
playing the 3rd part of this song.

Lesson 49

Exercise 1

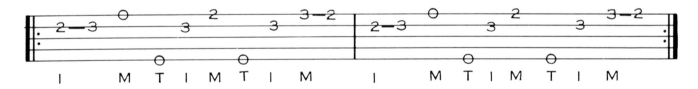

Exercise 2

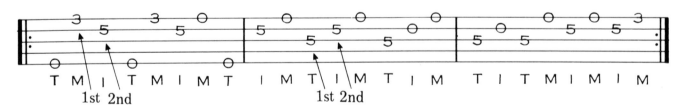

Exercise 3

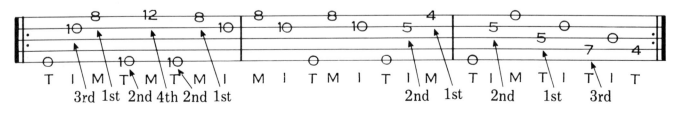

Exercise 4

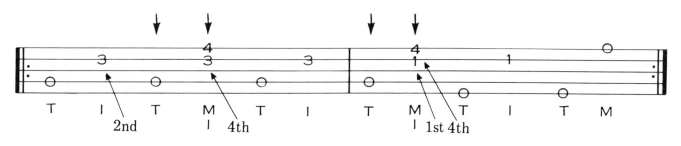

L'il Dave (Part 3)

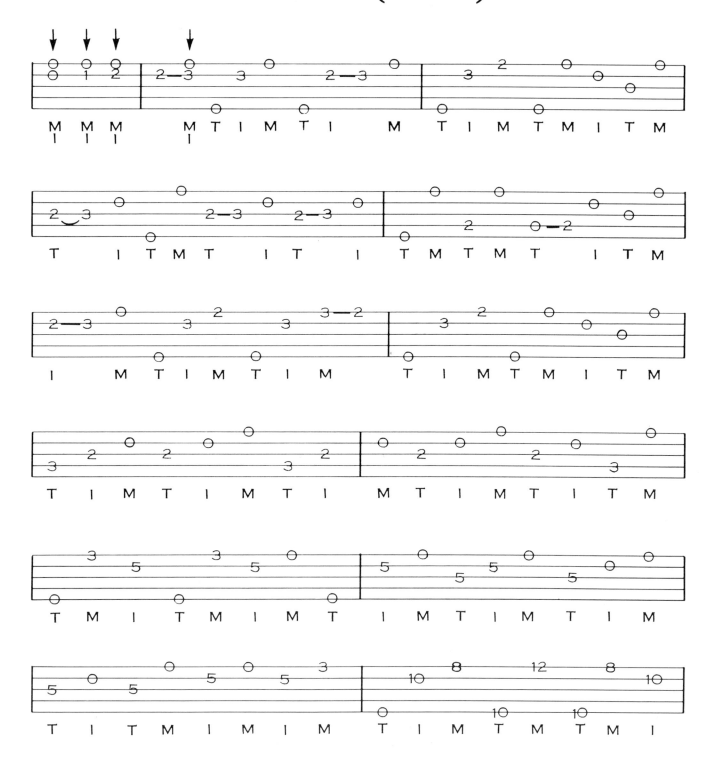

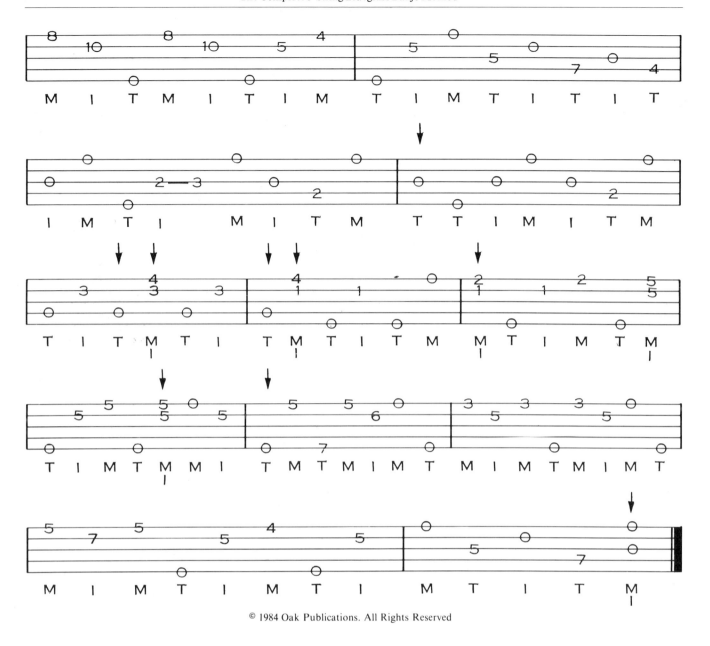

Lesson 50

Keep your 1st and 4th fingers in their positions, letting the 2nd and 3rd fingers do the moving around.

Exercise 1

Your last lesson is played in the key of D without a capo, something you won't see done very often. Start by tuning your 5th string to A.

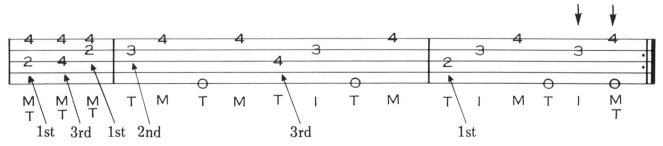

Exercise 2

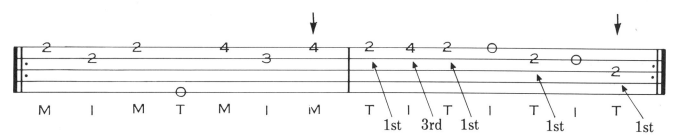

Exercise 3

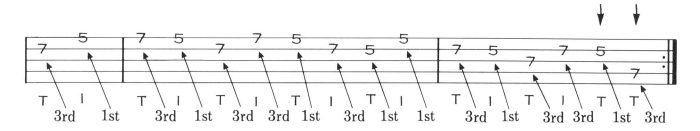

Exercise 4

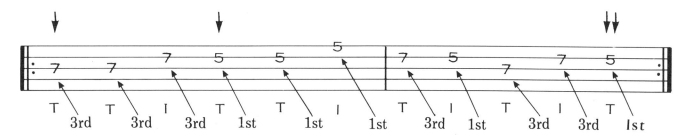

Arkansas Traveler

Traditional

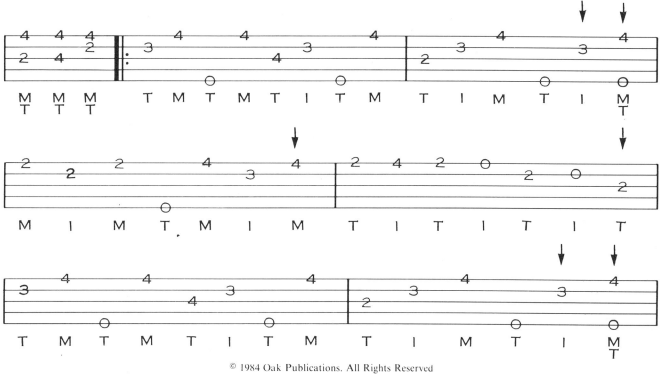

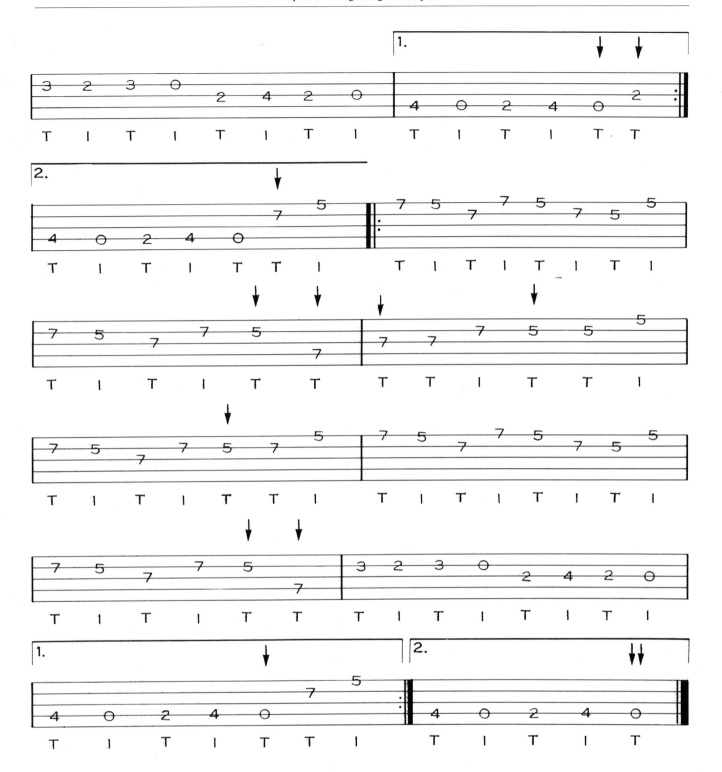